Por Amor al Pueblo: ¡Not Guilty!

Por Amor al Pueblo: ¡Not Guilty!

The Trial of the Winooski 44

Edited by

Ben Bradley
Nathan P. Hine
Judith Vollmann
Nancy Wasserman

Front Porch Publishing
1986

About the cover —

The cover illustration was drawn by an eleven-year-old Salvadoran refugee who is now living in Honduras. *Reubicados* translates "the relocated people." This drawing came to us from expert witness, Dr. Philippe Bourgois, Assistant Professor of Anthropology, Washington University, St. Louis, Missouri.

First Edition
Printed at Capital City Press, Montpelier, Vermont
Typeset at Type II, Hanover, New Hampshire

Library of Congress Number: 86-82607

ISBN: 0-9617504-0-5

Ordering inquiries should be addressed to:

Front Porch Publishing
RR 2, Box 281
White River Junction, Vermont 05001

Acknowledgements

Front Porch Publishing wishes to express gratitude for the generosity of the following benefactors, whose funding support made this book possible:

Boehm Foundation
William Drake
Anne Slade Frey
The Friendship Fund
The Occom Family Fund
Anne Pomeroy

We would like to express our appreciation to the following individuals who helped make this book a reality:

Andy Behrens, computer assistance
Alan Berolzheimer, proofreading
Marian Cox, typing
Kate Emlen, cover design
Melrose E. Huff, proofreading
Cheryl Jones, typing
Michael King, computer facilities
New Victoria Publishers, paste-up assistance
Marie LaPre-Grabon, page design
Merry Leonard, proofreading
Nellie Pennington, editorial consulting and proofreading
Jim Schley, editorial consulting
Liz Trott, map design

We would also like to thank Erinn Cafferty, Nicolette Corrao, Mary Koen, Calen Hine Pennington and Jim Schley for their continued support and encouragement. In particular, we thank Nellie Pennington for her ongoing vision and for all the ways in which she made this book possible.

Finally, we would like to thank the defendants whose conscientious actions inspired the testimony presented here.

Contents

Editors' Note

On March 26th, 1984, the fourth anniversary of the assassination of Oscar Romero, the Archbishop of El Salvador, two hundred people walked into United States Senator Robert Stafford's office in Winooski, Vermont. They had come, on the eve of a critical Senate vote on escalation of the contra war in Nicaragua, with two requests: that he stop voting for military aid to Central America and that he hold a public meeting on that issue. He refused. Three days later, still in his office, forty-four people were arrested and charged with illegal trespass. In November 1984, they were brought to trial by the State of Vermont. Twenty-six of the Defendants entered a plea of not guilty on the grounds that they were trying to prevent a greater harm: the U.S.-sponsored war against the people of Central America. In legal terms, this is called a necessity defense.

This book is the edited transcript of the trial of the Winooski 44. Through their own testimony and the testimony of Central American refugees and other expert witnesses the Defendants put the Reagan administration's Central America war policy on trial. Their acquittal, by a jury of twelve Vermonters, attests to the power and eloquence of the defense testimony.

The testimony has been edited to remove extraneous and repetitive sections and to improve its readability without altering the spirit and substance of the trial. A number of motions, continuances, objections, and cross-examinations have been omitted, along with some of the argument related to the technicalities of Vermont's trespassing law. Because of the repetitive nature of the State's evidence we chose to summarize it. Those who wish to study a more complete legal framework of the trial than is contained in the Appendices should write to Front Porch Publishing for a copy of the legal briefs and arguments which were not included here.

We give you this book because we believe the information it contains should be known by the United States people. It is a call to act as the Winooski 44 did, in defense of our neighbors to the south.

Ben Bradley
Nate Hine
Judith Vollmann
Nancy Wasserman

Introduction

Warning: The U.S. government would prefer that you not read the following pages. Reading them will expose you to pain and suffering, governmental cruelties, and cover-ups.

On the other hand, reading them may be good for your health. It may even constitute a small but important step in the struggle to help preserve and improve the health of people in El Salvador, Nicaragua, Guatemala, Honduras, Costa Rica and elsewhere. And if it has these results it will be good for the health of our country, a country which is presently suffering from the diseases of interventionism, nuclearism and "America-is-Number-One"-ism, a U.S. variant of the deadly "Deutschland Über Alles" disease of an earlier period.

If my optimism concerning the potential effects of this small book seems unwarranted, it stems from what happened in the courtroom whose proceedings it records. One would think that it would have been impossible to hear these grim stories spelled out day after day without being plunged into despair. Yet it turned out that they had an opposite effect. Incredibly, they carried an energizing message of hope.

How can I possibly say this? Because that is the effect they had not just on me as a defendant, but on everyone I have talked with who sat through the trial. And because that was the effect they had on the jurors, as they wiped the tears from their eyes, pondered the realities that had produced the tears, and came to a unanimous verdict of "Not Guilty."

Let me say a few words about the jurors. Ramsey Clark told me that when he looked over at them from the witness box, he had the impression that a majority of them had probably voted a few days earlier for the re-election of Ronald Reagan (under whose administration most of the crimes and lies exposed in the trial had taken place). True or not, Burlington, Vermont, where the proceedings took place, has a population of thirty thousand. It would have been pretty difficult for any of the jurors to have had any recent history of expressing *any* serious sentiments against U.S. foreign policy without its having come to the attention of the defendants or their acquaintances. Yet the defendants and their lawyers, in extensive pre-trial investigations of the jury panel, could find no instances in which any of them were known to have in any way had any personal connection with or expressed any sympathy for any of the anti-war activities of the months and years preceding the trial. The prosecution discovered no such "taint" in any of them. To complete the picture, all the defendants signed a pre-trial affidavit that they had heard the order to leave Senator Stafford's office and the warning that to continue their sit-in was a violation of the trespassing law. We did not challenge that law. Yet after hearing the testimony that is presented in the following pages, the jurors declared the defendants not guilty. They accepted the defendants' defense of necessity — that it was as necessary for us to "trespass" in Senator Stafford's office as it would be to "trespass" in a burning building to save the lives of its sleeping occupants.

When they pronounced this verdict, the jurors rejected both the narrow legalism of the prosecution's case and the media-trumpeted lies of the government concerning its activities and goals in Central America. They validated the hope the defendants had proclaimed by entering Senator Stafford's office and refusing to leave when threatened with arrest if they did not. They confirmed our hypothesis that the carefully planned and explained conscientious actions of a few ordinary citizens can open the eyes and hearts of other ordinary citizens. And that they can accomplish this even in the days of Ronald Reagan, whose deceptive TV geniality and "Good guys — Bad guys" Hollywood script contribute to the spread and virulence of the aforementioned diseases. In this way, such actions begin the process of reversing the present tide of cruelty and consent. They begin to heal the life-threatening disease of subservience to authority, restoring the power of victims and bystanders to resist.

Two qualifications about the process of change need to be made. The first is that it happens best when the actions are carried out not just without resorting to physical violence but with the Gandhian understanding that the participants have opponents but no enemies. To this I would add, in the spirit of Martin Luther King, Jr., that every opponent is a potential ally and is treated as such. Whatever reservations some of the participants in this action may have had about the ultimate applicability of this approach to all situations, it was the spirit we all followed to the best of our abilities, from the first phone calls and visits to Senator Stafford's office through the sit-in and its aftermath. In this case, we were rewarded not only by the effect on the jury but by the changes in Senator Stafford's voting pattern on Central America, which turned him from an opponent into an ally.

The second qualification is that the process of change is maddeningly slow at this point. Battles — and lives — are still being lost. One has only to think of the contras' policy of rape, torture, mutilation and murder, and of the June 1986 House vote in favor of aid; and to contrast this vote with the same Congress' treatment of the poor in this country — the children, the women, the farmers, the homeless, the sick, the disabled, the aged, the racial minorities, etc. (Do I need to list them all?) Most of all, millions of such people need basic changes in the economic principles and power relationships of our society. But meanwhile funding for the programs that might alleviate their daily lot is being diverted to military and paramilitary institutions and activities, a gigantic welfare boondoggle for the rich and powerful. In addition, the horrendous crimes in El Salvador that are herein described — from individual disappearances to massive assaults by bombing and strafing — continue, while the U.S. refuses to accept Salvadoran refugees (and similar refugees from other Central American countries) who have fled for their lives. Instead, it ships them back, now doubly marked, to face fates too horrible to contemplate.

Despite all this, it is important to note that even though the recent vote on contra aid was lost in the House (as I write, the vote in the Senate is still a few weeks away), polls taken that week indicate that the public opposed the measure by more than two-to-one. This tells us something about our supposed democracy, in which the pressures of arms manufacturers and other powerful interests can override the best instincts of a clear majority of the citizens. Clearly the power of money and of a money-dominated and money-hungry media plays a major, undemocratic role in deciding both who is elected and how they act after election. Clearly we will not have genuine political democracy until we have economic democracy.

The size of the public's opposition to aid for the contras also tells us that, contrary to the impression created by the mass media, the process of public enlightenment and incipient revolt is indeed getting underway all over the country. I saw additional evidence of this in the flood of phone calls and letters received by me and other defendants after the verdict. Besides offering their congratulations, many of them told of similar actions in their areas. I also see corroborative evidence in my travels and contacts in virtually all of the fifty-one states.

Why do the media downplay this reality? At least in part because they themselves are both owned by and beholden to multi-million-dollar special-interest corporations. NBC, for instance, is owned by General Electric, which manufactures the Gatling guns that are mounted on helicopters and used to mow down civilians in El Salvador. (Each Gatling gun fires five thousand bullets a minute.) General Electric has a short-sighted stake in preserving the unjust status quo — in Central America and in the United States. And whatever their occasional disagreements with an incumbent administration, they learned from the anti-Vietnam-War movement to fear the effects of an aroused and active populace. That movement opened visions of a new society, with changed attitudes and relationships, among human beings, between human beings and the other creatures, and between human beings and the world of Nature — earth, air, water, rain forests, and so forth.

It is impossible to predict at what point the present process of protest and of the affirmation of alternative values will culminate in a critical mass of morally outraged citizens who will no longer permit the U.S. government to engage in the lies, murders and insults to human dignity of its present policies. But it will surely happen if more and more people join the process of raising their consciousnesses and following their consciences, as, for all our limitations, the defendants, lawyers, witnesses and jurors in the Winooski 44 trial did. By educating, acting and voting in accord with our own common sense and our sometimes submerged instincts of universal sisterhood and brotherhood, we will speed up the day when it will happen. It will happen just as surely as an aroused public forced the government to withdraw its troops and bombers from Vietnam.

How can I explain these things? I can't. But I can suggest that it has something to do with the fact that the truth really does make people free. And apparently that includes even (perhaps especially) terrible, initially dismaying truth of the kind that is revealed in these pages. That is the kind of truth that we usually try to hide from, in a short-sighted effort to pursue our everyday lives with a moderate amount of surface tranquility.

Does the government know that the truth makes people free? There is considerable evidence that they do and that that is why they tell so many lies. One can read in the text, for example, that the U.S.-sponsored radio station in Honduras broadcast to the Nicaraguan people scurrilous tales about the terrible side effects of anti-malaria pills — that "children may become crazy" that "the malaria pills were from Russia and were for brainwashing" that swallowing them "could make you into a Communist." Here it is clear that they were afraid that the truth would allow the Nicaraguan people to become free of malaria — and, I suppose, continue to support the government that has brought them this blessing. For the same reason, the contras seek out medical workers and teachers for execution, the new medical centers and schools for burning.

One can also read the testimony of former CIA operatives who tell of that agency's practice of inventing lies and placing them in U.S. newspapers to deceive the public and win support for policies they would reject if they knew the truth.

Sadly, it seems likely that the government does know that the truth makes people free — as it freed the jury from their illusions about the government's role in Central America and from their prejudices against people who sit in at the offices of a duly-elected official. Tragically that is why government officials tell so many lies — sometimes even telling them to themselves in order to resist their own better instincts, which never completely disappear.

In conclusion, the jurors' verdict tells us a number of important facts. One is that our vaunted "free press" has failed to communicate to the public the realities of the policies being carried out by the U.S. government and its surrogates in Central America. When you read the testimony of Philippe Bourgois you will see a flagrant (but commonplace) instance of how executives of NBC and the *New York Times* made a conscious decision to censor important news that the public had a right and need to know.

A second, more hopeful fact is that when the public learns the truth about those policies it is horrified by them and votes against them, as the jury clearly did. The ideals for which the United States claims to stand, but which it cruelly violates, still lurk beneath the surface of our society, in the hearts of its citizens.

Third, there is a reason why most prosecutors and judges collaborate to deny political defendants the right to present evidence concerning the context in which they have acted. To return to the example of some passersby who discover a house in flames and know (or even suspect) that there are people sleeping inside, suppose they break through a locked door or window to rescue the occupants. Does anyone think that they would be arrested and charged with the "crime" of trespassing? If they were, does anyone think that they would be denied the right to explain the reasons for their actions? Yet this is the common practice in political trials in this country. It was, for instance, what happened to the church people in Arizona who were accused of criminally providing sanctuary to refugees from U.S.-supported terrorism in Central America. In such cases, the defendants are effectively denied the right to defend themselves.

Because this denial is commonplace in U.S. courts, I want to thank both the prosecutor, Kevin Bradley, and the judge, Frank Mahady, for agreeing to our use of the necessity defense. By doing so they upheld the Constitution and allowed us to exercise our right to a fair trial.

When you read the text, you will see that all of us also owe a great deal of gratitude to the lawyers and witnesses for their superb contributions to bringing out the truths of what is happening in Central America and of why and how the defendants responded by means of their actions. By "all of us," I do not mean just the defendants. I mean everyone who is interested in the truth and who by hearing or reading these particular truths has become or will become a little more free.

Finally, I want to suggest that when people become free, they begin to act from their deepest impulses of human unity, of love and caring. And this process of individual and societal healing works in the other direction as well. When people act on the inner stirrings that tell them of human familyhood, of fulfillment through love and caring, respect and compassion, they begin to become free. This is not the kind of freedom that seeks power over other individuals or power for one's own society to dominate and control other societies. It does not permit us to exploit other people. And it does not come from the barrel of a gun. But it is a freedom that causes strange and wonderful things to happen, if only on the very small scale of what happened in Senator Stafford's office and in the ensuing trial.

I do not mean to exaggerate the significance of these events but I do hope that publication of this book will extend their impact a little further, into the hearts and lives of a few more people.

David Dellinger

Peacham, Vermont
July 7, 1986

The credibility of the witnesses, the believability, if you will, of the witnesses, and the weight to be attached to their testimony, are entirely matters for your sound, practical judgment as fair-minded men and women.

Judge Frank A. Mahady

Defendants

Eric Broque
David Dellinger
Philip Fiermonte
Annie Gaillard
Joy Hammond
Melrose Huff
Jeanne Keller
Sylvia Lane
Robin Lloyd
Jeani Lowell
Paul Markowitz
Gil McCann
Joseph Moore
Celia Oyler
Jean Pineo
Nancy Powell
Joanna Rankin
Rose Reilly
John Rogers
Gary Sisco
Jennifer Strickler
Barr Swennerfelt
Lea Terhune
John Van Raalte
Nicholas Velvet
Abby Yasgur

Counsel For the State of Vermont

Kevin Bradley
Karen Shingler

Counsel For the Defense

Sandra Baird
Joan Bauer
Leslie Black
William Dorsch
John McCullough
Olin McGill
William Nelson
Linda Vance

Opening Statements

In chambers, November 13th, 1984, nine-thirty a.m.

WILLIAM DORSCH: There is a potential problem with space in the courtroom right now.

THE COURT: Yes, I'm aware of that.

MR. DORSCH: We would like that the spectators not be excluded. If necessary, people are willing to stand around the walls.

THE COURT: I'm perfectly willing to have people stand around.

MR. DORSCH: We have filed a motion with respect to the names of witnesses. I mentioned the other day that there would be one witness conceivably who would appear and would need his face masked. This is not at issue. He will not be here. But there are two witnesses who for reasons of safety of family at home, are very concerned about using their actual names. And they would like to use pseudonyms.

The only concern I have got is that I assume that if the Court granted our motion then we would not reveal to the jury that they were using pseudonyms. I assume — would that be the State's position?

KAREN SHINGLER: Well, it was my understanding in quickly reading the motion and the accompanying memorandum that you were going to make the jury aware of the fact that these people were testifying under pseudonyms.

MR. DORSCH: That's what we said in the brief. However, if there is going to be a disclosure that they used pseudonyms, then we're going to have to tell the jury why they're using pseudonyms. We're perfectly willing to have them testify without revealing that, because the thrust of their testimony goes to what they have been part of and been exposed to in Central America and the personal atrocities that they have had to be a part of. And they will also testify about their personal danger and the danger to their family.

THE COURT: Okay, then: the motion is granted that they may testify using pseudonyms, but the fact that they are using pseudonyms will not be mentioned. Okay?

MR. DORSCH: Thank you.

Open court, afternoon of November 13th. The jury was brought in.

THE COURT: Very well. Ms. Shingler?

Opening Statement for the State of Vermont:

MS. SHINGLER: My name is Karen Shingler. I'm a deputy state's attorney.

We're here because the State of Vermont has charged the twenty-six Defendants individually with unlawful trespass; specifically, that on March 26th of this year they were in Senator Stafford's office in Winooski, an office that is located on the fourth floor of the Champlain Mill in Winooski, and that they were asked to leave after having stayed there for some period of time. They were asked to leave by Ray Pecor who is the owner of the Champlain Mill. They were asked to leave by Rey Post who is Senator Stafford's staff director. They were also asked to leave by two members of the Winooski police force, a Detective Michael Spaulding and Patrolman Barry Lawrence.

I'd like to give you some background. At about noon on March 23rd, that being a Friday, approximately a hundred and fifty demonstrators gathered outside of the Winooski Mall. This demonstration had been arranged and the demonstrators had notified both Mr. Pecor and Mr. Post of their intentions.

About an hour and a half later, at approximately one-thirty on Friday of March 23rd, many of those one hundred fifty entered the Champlain Mill, proceeded up to the fourth floor, and went to greet Rey Post at the Senator's office. Rey Post, knowing they were coming, had spoken to the Senator, had indicated what the demands of the protesters were, and he as well as the Senator had formulated a statement to be given to the protesters upon their arrival on Friday the 23rd.

This exchange occurred, and this group of individuals appeared unsatisfied with the statement that Senator Stafford had offered to them. They had two demands: that Senator Stafford was not to support military aid to Central America and that Senator Stafford was, as soon as possible, to convene a public meeting. Senator Stafford responded with a brief history of his votes on the Central America issue and stated that he was willing to gather with certain representatives of this group to discuss their problems and the issues at hand. The group was unsatisfied with Senator Stafford's responses, and they indicated to Rey Post that they were going to stay in the Senator's office. Rey Post said okay and proceeded to slowly remove his staff from the office. By this time it was approximately three, three-thirty in the afternoon and Senator Stafford's office was preparing to close down as in the normal course of business.

At approximately five, five-fifteen, Rey Post, as the last staff member present, left, indicating to the protesters, "I'm leaving. Senator Stafford's office is closed. Goodbye." He did not lock the doors. He did not turn off the lights. He left this group of individuals in the Senator's office. Throughout the weekend the sit-in continued.

I take you now to Monday morning, March 25th, eight-thirty: the commencement of business hours at Senator Stafford's office. Rey Post arrives. They won't let him in his office, this group of individuals. Rey Post asks these individuals to please let him into his office and they say no. They demand a further statement from the Senator, and there is a little coming and going between Rey Post and the group of individuals as to how he is going about getting the statement if he can't get into his office. Rey Post comes back at approximately eleven-thirty in the morning and accompanying him is Ray Pecor and members of the Winooski Police Department. Rey Post conveys to the Defendants Senator Stafford's final response: that Senator Stafford is willing to meet with a specified group of individuals and once again states his record on certain rulings in the Senate with regard to Central America. The Defendants again express some anger or some dissatisfaction with Senator Stafford's response and once again they ask Rey Post, "Please, you have to talk to the Senator one more time."

Rey Post goes back, confers with the Senator who is in Washington. He comes back and says, "On behalf of the Senator and on behalf of myself, you have to leave. We cannot conduct business. You're violating the rights of citizens of the State of Vermont for access to their Senator." Accompanying him is Ray Pecor. Ray Pecor identifies himself as the owner of the Champlain Mill and indicates to the Defendants, "Please leave. Senator Stafford would like you to leave. You have been here all weekend. We have let you do what you want. You have to leave now." Some individuals leave. The Defendants remain in Senator Stafford's office.

A member of the Winooski police force, Michael Spaulding, says to the remaining group, "If you do not leave, you will be placed under arrest." They remained, and they were arrested by members of the Winooski Police Department as well as members of the Vermont State Police.

As this trial goes forward, you may be hearing something that lawyers call the necessity defense. It is my understanding that the focus of this necessity defense will be on Central America. Ladies and gentlemen, it really doesn't matter what you feel about Central America; and ladies and gentlemen, it does not matter what the Defendants feel about Central America. There may be things you will hear that may be upsetting about what is going on in Central America, things you may not like, things I may not like, things apparently the Defendants did not like when they heard them. Ladies and gentlemen, all I'm asking is that you please focus on our roles here throughout the rest of the week; that we're here because the Defendants broke the laws of the State of Vermont. We're not here for any other reason.

I'm confident, ladies and gentlemen, that you will find that the State has satisfied its burden that on March 26th of this year, twenty-six individuals who are sitting on the other side of this courtroom were in Senator Stafford's office, were asked to leave by Rey Post, by Ray Pecor, by Michael Spaulding and by Barry Lawrence. They chose not to, and I submit to you, ladies and gentlemen of the jury, to return a verdict of guilty. Thank you.

Opening Statement for the Defense:

MR. DORSCH: As the attorney for the Defendants, I guess my reaction to what you have just heard is, well, why did twenty-six people do that?

What the State has told you are the facts that would appear to satisfy you that these twenty-six people should all be convicted of unlawful trespass. I assume that they will ask you to ignore anything else happening, anything else in the Defendants' minds and to assume that the Defendants were headstrong, were irrational, or made this unexplainable decision.

As the trial proceeds, it will be the Defendants' opportunity to present their case. And we're going to present that case through several of these twenty-six people. You will understand that they are not irrational. They are people of peace. They are people concerned. They are worried about their children. They're worried about their country. They're worried about other people, and they will explain all that to you.

We're also going to present a number of expert witnesses for you to listen to, people who are well versed and very, very knowledgeable on Latin American affairs, on the killing, the bombing, the maiming, the torture, the death squads, all of the things that are of great concern to the people of this country.

They will talk to you about the importance of Senator Stafford, his importance in the Senate in crucial votes on Central America. You will understand as the trial proceeds why these people have done what they have done and why it is important and why it was a necessity.

The evidence with respect to the problems in Central America you will only hear after the State's case has ended. It's very important that you keep an open mind. The Defendants will tell you and will show you that there was a necessity for them to do what they did; that they were acting on behalf of themselves, their children, their country, people of Central America and us. We're confident that at the end of this trial you will return a verdict of not guilty with respect to every one of the Defendants, because you will understand and you will see from the witnesses and the evidence presented that these people did something within the lawful authority of the United States and the State of Vermont. Thank you.

THE COURT: Thank you, Mr. Dorsch.

As I'm sure you folks are aware, it's important that you avoid any kind of knowledge about this case, the issues involved in this case or anything other than what you hear in the courtroom. And there obviously will be some media attention to this particular case. So I urge you to avoid radio news broadcasts, television broadcasts and with regard to the newspapers, if you could have a friend or family member go through it for you before you see it, you can describe in general terms what you don't want to see, and they can go through with a pair of snippers and snip it for you. But you can see the rest of what is going on in the world and if you're really interested they can save the clippings for you, and you can see them later. If you could, be very, very careful about that.

Also, you shouldn't discuss the case with anybody, even among yourselves at this point. We will give you all the time you want to do that later. You shouldn't discuss it with anyone. If anyone does come up to you and try to discuss the case with you, you should politely but firmly tell them you just can't do it. And I know that's hard to do, because that happens to me fairly frequently. People quite innocently come up to me and with the best of intentions mention a case to me that I shouldn't be hearing about from anybody. I know it's hard to do, because I find it hard to do; to politely but firmly tell them that, sorry, but that's what we have to do and we really appreciate your cooperation. If inadvertently something comes to your attention, let me know about it in the form of a note to the court officer. What I'll do is share that with counsel and then we'll want to visit with you maybe about it and see where we go from there. If you could let me know if something like that does happen, just as soon as you can, I'd appreciate it. I would like to comment that today has been a long day for everybody, especially in this hot room. You folks are excused. See you a little before nine in the morning, and we'll get started promptly at nine.

Summary of the State's Evidence

Open court, November 14, 1984, nine-thirty a.m.

The state presented its evidence. The following is a summary.

Rey Post, director of the Senator's six-person Vermont staff, testified first. He stated that two Defendants visited him several days before the occupation to describe to him the upcoming event and the requests the protesters would be making of Senator Stafford. Mr. Post relayed these requests (he called them "demands" although he admitted that the protesters never used that word) to the Senator at this point and on several later occasions.

At about one p.m. on Friday, March 23rd, according to Mr. Post and other prosecution witnesses, one hundred and fifty people crammed themselves into Senator Stafford's office, overflowing into the common area outside. "Several individuals began to weave a web of yarn throughout the entire office in what they called a Web of Life." There was some discussion between Mr. Post and the protesters and an exchange of telecopied messages with the Senator in Washington, and the staff left the office early that afternoon (after locking up some "sensitive documents" and disconnecting the telephones) while fifty to sixty members of the group remained.

On Monday morning, Mr. Post returned with representatives of the Winooski and State Police, the U.S. Marshall, and Raymond Pecor, the owner of the building. They were greeted by two spokespeople who informed them that the office had been renamed for "a little girl in Central America who had been assassinated." The office, they were told, had been "turned into a new kind of facility for exchange of views on Central America." The fifty to one hundred people present in the office that morning refused to leave unless the Senator agreed to a public meeting to discuss U.S. policy in Central America.

It seemed clear to Mr. Post and Mr. Pecor that it was impossible for the Senator's staff to conduct business in the office. Mr. Post, Mr. Pecor, and Winooski Police Detective Michael Spaulding testified that they each addressed the group occupying the office and asked the group to leave, warning the occupiers that they would be arrested and charged with trespass if they remained. After the last of these warnings, the group was given ten minutes to leave the office. A spokesperson circulated among the "affinity groups" (Officer Spaulding used this term) and some of those present took the opportunity and left at that point. Patrol Officer Barry Lawrence of the Winooski Police Department informed those who remained that they were under arrest for criminal trespass. These forty-four people were then arrested and removed from Senator Stafford's office by Winooski and Vermont State Police Department officers and taken to the Colchester State Police Barracks.

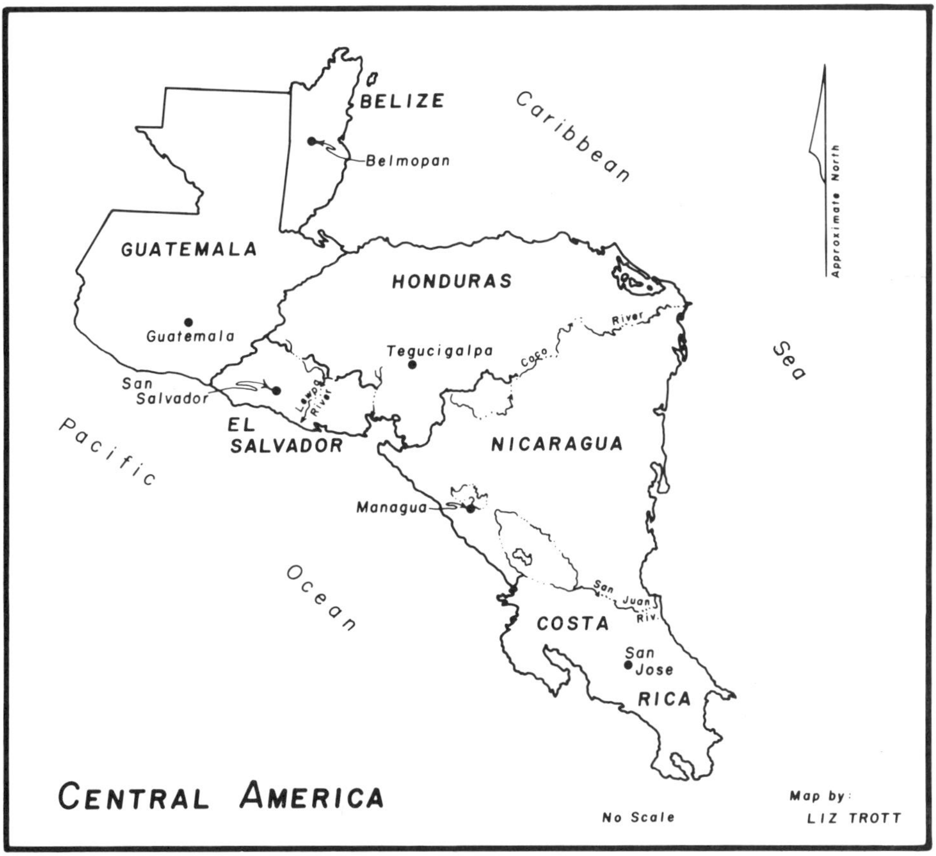
BELIZE
Belmopan
Caribbean
Sea
Approximate North
GUATEMALA
Guatemala
HONDURAS
Tegucigalpa
Coco
River
San
Salvador
Lempa
River
EL
SALVADOR
NICARAGUA
Pacific
Ocean
Managua
San
Juan
Riv.
COSTA
RICA
San
Jose
CENTRAL AMERICA
No Scale
Map by:
LIZ TROTT

Defense Testimony

THE COURT: Defendants' first witness?

MS. BAIRD: Mr. Philip Fiermonte.

PHILIP FIERMONTE, being duly sworn, testified as follows:

Direct Examination by Mr. Dorsch:

Q. You are Philip Fiermonte?

A. Yes, I am.

Q. And you are a Defendant in this case?

A. Yes, I am.

Q. And can you tell the jury where you live?

A. I live in Burlington, Vermont.

Q. And you are appearing here to testify to the jury today about work you have done with an organization in the area?

A. That's right.

Q. Can you tell the jury what that organization's name is?

A. Burlington CASA. The Central America Solidarity Association.

Q. And can you tell the jury what kind of work you have done locally with that organization?

A. Well, for the past three-and-a-half years, I have been a member of that organization, an active leader, and we have conducted a number of forums throughout the area, basically educating the public about the situation in Central America. We are opposed to the present U.S. policy in Central America. One of the responsibilities that I had was as one of two representatives of Vermont to three national networks: the Committee in Solidarity with the People of El Salvador, the Network in Solidarity with the Nicaraguan People, and the Network in Solidarity with the People of Guatemala. These are national organizations. There are over four hundred chapters of these organizations throughout the country.

Q. I show you this document. Can you tell us what it is?

A. Yes. This is a map of Central America.

Q. Are you familiar with the geographic area of Central America?

A. Yes, I am.

Q. Then, can you tell the jury what different countries you're talking about that are the focus of —

A. Well, our concerns have to do with the entire region of Central America, particularly the military aid from the United States to the governments of El Salvador and Guatemala, two of the most repressive countries in the world, where over sixty thousand civilians have been murdered in the last five years. Our concern also has to do with Nicaragua, located here, and the U.S. funding of groups that are trying to overthrow the Nicaraguan government. They are based in Honduras, which is here. I might add there are eight U.S. airfields in Honduras and it's strategically located in that it borders on Guatemala, El Salvador, and Nicaragua.

Q. Now, Phil, I'd like to focus your attention on the period of time prior to March 26th, 1984, several months prior to that time. Can you tell us what work you were doing with respect to Central America?

A. In December of 1983, a number of peace groups in the Burlington area, including Burlington CASA, met and formed a coalition called The Coalition Against U.S. Intervention in Central America. And it was our feeling that there was a great threat of increased escalation of U.S. military involvement in Central America and that we needed to work together as a coalition to take action to stop that escalation.

Q. Now, what basis did you have for that information?

A. Well, we are all students of the situation in Central America. At that time, there were reports of increased military aid to El Salvador and Guatemala. In Honduras, there was a massive escalation of U.S. military presence. I mentioned the eight bases that the United States was building in Honduras. There were a large number of troops being deployed to Honduras.

Q. What actions, if any, did your organization plan to take in response to this buildup?

A. Well, initially, we planned a contingency plan if there was any direct military intervention in Central America. As time went on and as news came out about Central America, we felt that it was important that we take some sort of direct action in the very near future to call attention to the atrocities in Central America and to help stop U.S. intervention in Central America; and that was the beginning of the planning for the activity at Senator Stafford's office.

Q. Can you tell the jury what happened as the winter progressed and you got towards March of 1984?

A. We decided that Senator Stafford, as a Republican and long-time supporter of the administration's policy in Central America, was someone that we thought we could influence on Central America.

Q. Now, Phil, can you tell us if there was any particular reason that you felt Senator Stafford was an important person to approach?

A. Well, I talked with people in the national network and the feeling was that because Senator Stafford was a Republican, he was a key person. He seemed to be a moderate Republican, but had supported the administration in Central America and if he moved away from the administration's policies, that could potentially affect other Republicans. And I think it's important to say that we had met with Senator Stafford before and had communicated with him a number of times. At one point in 1982 at a meeting we had, Senator Stafford indicated to us that Central America was not an area of major concern for him, or major expertise, and he said he only knows what he reads in the papers. So, given that, we felt that he would be someone who could be swayed with information and activity.

Q. And did you undertake to convey that information to him?

A. Yes. In the three-and-a-half years of my involvement, we have done a lot of lobbying and have communicated information and our concerns to Senator Stafford on a number of occasions.

Q. Can you tell the jury what happened as you got closer to March 26th in terms of the planning of what was going to go on over that weekend?

A. We knew that March was a critical time in terms of U.S. escalation, and all the national networks were encouraging local groups throughout the country to take part in educational and other activities around Central America. In fact, this week that I'm talking about, Central America Week, was a week of focused activity throughout the country. In all my experience with Central America, that was the week of most concentrated lobbying and education and protest action.

Q. Could you tell the jury what kind of activities were going on?

A. In Washington during that week, there was a national effort to draw attention to the situation in Central America. There was a national day of advocacy where literally thousands of people went to Washington to lobby their congresspeople. There was a national religious convocation in Washington at that time.

Q. Before we leave that, who organized and who was involved in the religious convocation for peace?

A. The one that played the most major role in organizing the activity was the Inter-Religious Task Force on Central America.

Q. And what group or groups comprise the Inter-Religious Task Force?

A. Virtually all denominations were involved with the Inter-Religious Task Force on Central America.

Q. You can proceed telling us about what was going on.

A. In Washington another major activity that was happening was that a labor organization, National Labor Committee in Support of Human Rights and Democracy in El Salvador, held a rally outside the Congress. This is an organization that consists of many of the presidents of the major labor unions throughout the United States. In virtually every major city in the country, there were rallies going on. Religious organizations organized a number of vigils and commemorative services for Archbishop Romero who was assassinated in El Salvador, I believe, three years before that date.

Q. Phil, as the weekend of March 24th through 26th approached, were there any particular activities in the United States Congress that were of concern to your organization?

A. One of the reasons that the national solidarity organizations worked to organize the events that occurred during Central America Week was that there were going to be some votes coming up in the spring on Central America and they thought it would be very important to have concentrated activity to influence those votes on Central America.

Q. Phil, is there any connection between the events that occurred in Senator Stafford's office the weekend in question and what was going on nationally?

A. Clearly there was. This activity was not in a vacuum. And the idea and the purpose were largely to influence votes that were coming up in the U.S. Congress. Suffice it to say that it's Congress that appropriates funds that go to El Salvador, Guatemala, and the Nicaraguan rebels.

Q. Mr. Fiermonte, did you accomplish anything, in your opinion, by your actions in Winooski?

A. Yes. Most significantly, Senator Stafford's position on aid to the contras, the group of people trying to overthrow the Nicaraguan government, changed. Initially, before our activity, he supported that aid to the contras. After our activity, he opposed it and voted against it. So, yes.

MR. DORSCH: I have nothing further.

THE COURT: Thank you, Mr. Dorsch. Mr. Bradley?

Cross-Examination by KEVIN BRADLEY:

Q. With respect to this particular incident on the 26th of March, when you were sitting in Senator Stafford's office, did you hear Mr. Pecor address the group and ask those of you in the room to leave the office?

A. Yes, I did.

Q. Did you hear Mr. Post, who was Senator Stafford's aide, ask everyone to leave the office?

A. Yes, I did.

Q. Did you hear Officer Michael Spaulding request that everyone leave and further, that if they did not leave, that they were subject to arrest?

A. Yes, I did.

Q. Did you hear Officer Barry Lawrence make that same address?

A. I believe I did, yes.

Q. Did you remain inside?

A. Yes, I did.

Q. Did you know that you were going to be arrested?

A. I assumed that I was, yes.

Q. What, at that time, was the final demand or request that those of you in Senator Stafford's office were making of Senator Stafford?

A. The request that Senator Stafford meet publicly with Vermonters over the issue of Central America.

Q. Did you understand from Mr. Post that Senator Stafford agreed to meet with you at some later date?

A. No. He did not agree to a public meeting in any sense. He said he would meet with a delegation. He said we could pick, I don't know if he said a number, but a small number of people to meet behind closed doors but no, he certainly did not agree to a public meeting.

Q. But he did agree to meet at least with a delegation of you at some later time?

A. Yes.

Q. If Senator Stafford, on March 26th, had dropped what he was doing in Washington, taken the next plane to Vermont and convened an open forum, would that have stopped the civil wars and the turmoil in Central America?

A. No.

MR. BRADLEY: I have no other questions.

THE COURT: Thank you, Mr. Bradley. Mr. Dorsch?

Re-Direct-Examination by MR. DORSCH:

Q. Phil, when you were in the office, in Senator Stafford's office, on Monday morning, did you feel you were there with legal authority?

A. Yes, I did.

Q. And did you ever feel you were there without lawful authority?

A. No.

MR. DORSCH: I have nothing further.

THE COURT: Thank you. Mr. Bradley?

Re-Cross-Examination by MR. BRADLEY:

Q. Yes, Your Honor. When Mr. Post, Mr. Pecor, Officer Michael Spaulding and also Officer Barry Lawrence asked you all to leave, and said that you would be subject to arrest if you don't leave, you still thought you were there with lawful authority?

A. Yes.

MR. BRADLEY: No questions, Your Honor.

THE COURT: Thank you, Mr. Bradley. Mr. Dorsch?

MR. DORSCH: I have no further questions, Your Honor.

THE COURT: Thank you very much. Ms. Baird?

SANDRA BAIRD: Sonia Hernandez. I might add she is a Spanish-speaking person and we have a translator.

THE COURT: Very well. I need Title 12 in the oath — Foreign Interpreter. Thank you. Please be seated. Your name, sir?

MARK McCAFFREY: Mark McCaffrey.

THE COURT: Very well. Could you tell us briefly your qualifications as an interpreter?

MR. McCAFFREY: I'm a former professor of Spanish and I have plenty of experience.

THE COURT: Would you raise your right hand, please, sir? Do you solemnly swear that you will justly and truly and yet impartially interpret the oath administered to the witness and the testimony that the witness shall give relative to the cause now under consideration, so help you God?

MR. McCAFFREY: I do.

THE COURT: Thank you very much, sir. Ms. Baird?

SONIA HERNANDEZ, having been duly sworn, testified as follows:

Direct Examination by MS. BAIRD:

Q. Ms. Hernandez, could you state your name?

A. Sonia Hernandez.

Q. How old are you?

A. Twenty-seven.

Q. Where do you live?

A. In New York.

Q. What do you do there?

A. I am working.

Q. Could you tell the jury what kind of work you do?

A. Cleaning houses. I also work on the refugee committee.

Q. Can you describe the refugee committee's work for the jury?

A. We're developing programs to seek solutions to the problems which Salvadoran refugees are experiencing here in the United States.

Q. Ms. Hernandez, are there a number of Salvadoran refugees in New York City?

A. Yes, I do not know the exact number, but there's a large quantity of Salvadorans. We are working in Westbury and Hampton and there are twenty-two thousand Salvadorans in those two cities on Long Island.

Q. What kinds of work do you do for them?

A. For the most part, we are spending our time developing health programs, trying to establish a health clinic to meet the medical needs and health needs of the Salvadorans we are serving. We are also gathering various necessities such as clothing and medicine to send to refugees in Honduras and Guatemala.

Q. Are there refugees in Nicaragua as well?

A. Yes, there are.

Q. Where are you originally from, Ms. Hernandez?

A. Morazán province.

Q. In what country?

A. El Salvador.

Q. Perhaps Ms. Hernandez could point out to the jury where she is from in El Salvador. There is a map right there.

A. (Indicated.)

Q. How long did you live in that village?

A. Twelve years.

Q. And where did you go at the age of twelve?

A. I went to Morazán proper town. There was no special education for seventh, eighth and ninth grade [in the village].

Q. Your travels managed to take you to San Salvador [capital of El Salvador] as well?

A. I went to San Salvador afterwards to study, take my high school studies and to study nursing.

Q. Did your family stay in the village in Morazán?

A. Yes, they stayed there until 1981.

Q. Ms. Hernandez, could you describe what your village in Morazán was like? For instance, what is the major occupation in that area?

A. For the most part, Morazán is a farming community, with the exception of the town proper which is more or less urban.

Q. Is this area a prosperous region? A poor region? How would you describe it?

A. It has been prosperous; that is, people were able to survive and do more than survive in the area as farmers. They were renters. They do not own the land.

Q. By renters, do you mean sharecroppers?

A. No. No, a small number of proprietors owned the land and they paid the farmers for working for them.

Q. Is that area still prosperous?

A. The vast majority of the villages were destroyed and leveled by bombardment in military offensives. At this point in time, the small village which I am from originally no longer exists.

Q. And how did that happen?

A. In 1980 and 1981 a terrible repression began against the farming population.

Q. Repression by whom?

A. Repression by the government and its military forces.

Q. What forms did that oppression take?

A. The military offensives are composed of so-called cleanup operations carried out on the presumed justification of the existence of guerrilla soldiers in given areas. The outcome of a military cleanup offensive is the destruction of towns and the death of civilians.

Q. Is this on the part of the government of El Salvador?

A. Yes.

Q. You say there are opposing guerrillas. Can you describe the guerrillas?

A. For many years a movement of increasingly organized resistance in opposition to the system of government in El Salvador has been growing, as it has always been and continues to be an extremely unjust system of government.

Q. And the opposition in your village had been growing, is that your testimony?

A. Yes. The farmers began to ask for increases in salaries, increases in pay, and were met with firearms and repression of the kind I have been describing.

Q. Is the church active in the formation of opposition?

A. Not really in the formation of opposition per se, though the church was in agreement that the existing system required change.

Q. And as a result of this growing opposition in 1980 and 1981, there were, you say, attacks on your village?

A. Yes.

Q. What happened to your family?

A. In one of these invasions, a great many civilians over the age of fifty were taken out of their houses and rounded up — those who could not run away, those over fifty-one, fifty-two years old — my father among them.

Q. What happened to your father?

A. They murdered him, burned him alive along with other elders like himself and children who were not fast enough to get out of the village in time.

Q. Was your father a guerrilla?

A. No. He was an old fifty-two-year-old man who had no idea at all about what that would be.

Q. At the time of this battle, Ms. Hernandez, where were you?

A. I was in San Salvador studying nursing. I didn't finish. They suspended me at the school.

Q. Did you continue to work in San Salvador?

A. Yes, the kind of work I did was to attend to the refugees in the refugee camps in San Salvador.

Q. What are these refugee camps in San Salvador? Can you describe them?

A. They were initiated by Archbishop Romero, who, in attention to the large numbers of countryside refugees coming to San Salvador, opened up the refugee camps.

Q. What is the purpose of refugee camps?

A. To give the thousands of farm workers displaced from their farms and their villages some shelter, a place to live, a place to survive.

Q. That's the church of El Salvador? They were helping in organizing these camps?

A. Yes. It is principally the church, with its various parishes, that has begun to create a program of refugee sanctuary, harboring of village refugees, in San Salvador.

Q. Is that what Archbishop Romero was active in?

A. Yes.

Q. Ms. Hernandez, were you in San Salvador when the Archbishop was assassinated?

A. Yes.

Q. Did you attend his funeral?

A. Yes.

Q. Can you describe the events of that funeral?

A. Six days after the death of Archbishop Monsignor Romero thousands of farm people, country people, gathered at the cathedral to bid their last farewell to the Archbishop. After all the people had gathered in the cathedral, a large shot, explosion, was heard and right after the loud shot or explosion, a great many people in the cathedral who were attending the funeral witnessed that directly across the street, from inside the national palace (which houses the Salvadoran army) soldiers were firing into the crowd.

Q. Were there deaths?

A. A great many. After everyone had left I went back and counted twenty-seven dead bodies. Just the same, I know a great many people, women, who left the cathedral running with dead children in their arms. It was a great and bloody ordeal with a lot of anguish for those present.

Q. How do you know that this was a government attack?

A. Because you could see the National Guard firing from up at the palace.

Q. Did you stay in San Salvador for a while after the death of the Archbishop?

A. Yes, I stayed there through the rest of 1980 and through 1981.

Q. And what was the atmosphere in San Salvador after the death of the Archbishop?

A. Great anger, but even greater anguish than anger, because Bishop Romero was a man who had offered a lot of hope, consolation and promise to the Salvadorans.

Q. Did the war in San Salvador continue?

A. Yes. There was a great deal of heavy fear and apprehension to the extreme at the funeral, within the processions and demonstrations of sympathy for Bishop Romero. It was discovered subsequently that a lot of people had been planted there to note civilians, take names, take photographs and a great many people disappeared as a result of that.

Q. When you say disappeared, what does that mean?

A. A great many homes are invaded and people removed from them. Subsequent to those kinds of operations the rest of the members of the family go into the streets of San Salvador the next day to look for the bodies of those who disappeared. Those bodies which are not found are counted as disappeared because no traces are found.

Q. Did there come a time when something happened to your fiancé? When was that?

A. In May of 1981. Despite all of the turmoil, I was determined to continue my relationship and get married. My fiancé was walking down the street one day and apparently at no provocation at all, several heavily armed men got out of a car. These men are known as the death squad and they savagely murdered my boyfriend at knifepoint, left him dismembered.

Q. How old was he?

A. Twenty years.

Q. What did he do for a living?

A. He was a student.

Q. Did you stay in San Salvador after that?

A. Yes, for the rest of 1981.

Q. Did you ever have access to your boyfriend's body? Was that ever found?

A. No, neither I, nor, I think, any of his family members ever had the courage to go and claim the body because that entailed danger since one is a marked person by going to claim a dead body.

Q. So, what was your life like after that in San Salvador?

A. Of course my life was shattered, but for a while I was able to join with friends who had suffered similar tragedies; that is, the loss of a brother, loss of a boyfriend, loss of some family members, and we managed to see each other through the next few months.

Q. Did events occur which caused you to decide to leave El Salvador, and what were they?

A. While I was still in San Salvador living with a lady who dearly loved me, I received a death-threatening phone call one night. They came to look for me one night. When they didn't find me, they took instead the seventeen-year-old son, one of two sons this lady had, and the only one who was home. The boy's intestines were — he was completely disemboweled. The lady more or less lost her mind. I understood, of course, that I was in imminent and crucial danger and that if I did nothing to try to save myself my chances were slim of carrying on.

Q. What did you do as a result of that evening?

A. Almost nothing. Nothing much one can do under those circumstances. No options, no alternatives for the simple reason that no one really wants to give shelter or harbor to someone over whose neck is hanging that kind of danger and stigma.

Q. Did you leave your country then?

A. I spent ten anguishing days going from one house to another, knowing that I was a curse to anyone's home. Those were ten terrifying days in which I lived very close to death. And it was amidst that situation, on the verge of madness myself, walking around alone in a war zone south of San Salvador, that I decided that the only thing for me to do was to leave my country.

Q. And at that time you left?

A. Sí. It is not as if I had any destination or particular direction in mind. The only thing that concerned me was to get out of El Salvador and so I did. The first place I went was Guatemala.

Q. You eventually went to Mexico as well?

A. In Guatemala, the situation was no different. The same kind of fear and repression permeated existence there, and so, seeing that, I decided to continue ahead to Mexico.

MS. BAIRD: Thank you very much.

THE COURT: Thank you very much. Ms. Shingler?

MS. SHINGLER: Thank you, Your Honor.

Cross-Examination by MS. SHINGLER:

Q. Good afternoon, Ms. Hernandez. My name is Karen Shingler. I'm a Deputy State Attorney. I'd like to discuss just a few brief questions. You've indicated on your direct testimony that there has been a great deal of fighting going on in El Salvador; is that correct?

A. Yes.

Q. And as far as you know, there's a great deal of fighting that is continuing right now in El Salvador?

A. The repression that I spoke of has continued the same, if not grown. It is possible to speak of a difference in form.

Q. So, would it be fair to say that for several years the fighting has not stopped?

A. Yes. And the example I was hoping to give was that not so many corpses are found in San Salvador as before but the number of disappeared is the same or higher.

Q. So, Ms. Hernandez, it's your opinion and belief as you and I speak right now that there is a state of civil war in El Salvador?

A. Yes, but I have a contradiction to offer with the term civil war. The people of El Salvador do not consider that they are involved in civil war, but rather as Archbishop Romero put it, it is a conflict between the people and the State.

MS. SHINGLER: Thank you very much.

THE COURT: Thank you, Ms. Shingler. Ms. Baird, anything further?

MS. BAIRD: I have nothing further.

THE COURT: Very well. Thank you very much, ma'am. The next witness?

WILLIAM NELSON: Annie Gaillard.

ANNIE GAILLARD, being duly sworn, testified as follows:

Direct Examination by MR. NELSON:

Q. Annie, would you state your full name and your address please?

A. Priscilla Ann Gaillard and I live in Walden, Vermont.

Q. What is your occupation?

A. I am a farmer and a mother.

Q. And are you one of the Defendants in this case?

A. Yes, I am.

Q. And I take it that you admit that you were in Senator Stafford's office; is that correct?

A. Yes.

Q. Can you explain to the jury what brought you to Senator Stafford's office?

A. I had heard a lot of information about what was going on in Central America which disturbed me a lot. I had written a few letters to Stafford trying to explain my position and I called him a few times and had gotten run-of-the-mill form letters that just basically said he went along with Reagan's policy in Central America and he didn't seem willing to go into it in any more personal way as to why he felt that he had to follow Reagan's policy.

Q. Can you tell us some of the things that you heard that were disturbing to you?

A. At the time I was six months pregnant and the things that I heard about happening to the children, that seventy-five per cent of the refugees were children, that at least half, sometimes three-quarters of —

MS. SHINGLER: Objection, Your Honor. I was going to wait and see what this was going to be. Seems to be all hearsay. Question calls for a hearsay answer.

THE COURT: Mr. Nelson?

MR. NELSON: Your Honor, it's not being offered for the truth, but to show the witness' reasonable understanding.

THE COURT: Well, relying on Mr. Justice Peck's language in *State v. Shotton*, testing what is reasonably conceived by the Defendant to have been a necessity, I will allow the question and the answer but with a caution for the jury that it is to be considered by them only as to the witness' reasonable perception of a situation of necessity and not for the truth of any of the matters asserted.

Q. Go on. You were, I think, in the middle of an answer.

A. Let's see. In a family of five children, three of them would probably die before the age of five through either malnutrition or murders or things like that. That the military will torture children to torture the parents who are made to watch. One instance I heard, through a Guatemalan refugee, was that the children were held by their ankles and swung around until their heads hit a wall or tree or something which killed them and the parents were made to watch this.

Q. This last one you say you heard from a Guatemalan refugee?

A. Yes, I did.

Q. How about the statistics that you were giving us earlier? Where did you get those from?

A. I think some of them were in books and also information groups like CASA.

Q. You say you have made efforts before this to contact the Senator?

A. Yes.

Q. How many such efforts did you make?

A. I would say there were probably two phone calls and two or three letters.

Q. And you found satisfactory responses to that?

A. No. It was just usually the form letter. If it was a phone call they would just ask what I was calling about and I would say what I was feeling and they would just say what's your name and your address and then that was all and about a week or two weeks later I would get the same form letter back.

Q. I think you told us briefly what brought you to Senator Stafford's office. What was your purpose in being there? What was your intention?

A. I guess I was feeling frustrated by not getting anywhere with writing, the usual way that you contact your elected officials, and this was like a last resort.

Q. You're a citizen of Vermont?

A. Yes, I am.

Q. And a constituent of the Senator's; is that right?

A. Yes.

Q. Did you feel that you had legal authority to be in his office during work hours?

A. Yes, I did.

MR. NELSON: No further questions.

THE COURT: Very well. Thank you, Mr. Nelson. Mr. Bradley?

MR. BRADLEY: Thank you, Your Honor.

Cross-Examination by MR. BRADLEY:

Q. Ms. Gaillard, when did the strife, the violence in El Salvador begin?

A. When did it begin?

Q. Yes.

A. God, it's been going on for years. The revolution or the government-against-the-people-type thing.

Q. It's been going on for years?

A. Yes, that's my understanding of it.

Q. Has it changed any since March 26th?

A. I don't think so unless the aid that our country gives fluctuates; that seems to affect the strife that's going on down there.

Q. Do you know when this country began giving aid to El Salvador?

A. Well, there's been some sort of military intervention in Central America way back, in the '20s and 1800s even.

Q. Do you know how much financial aid is given to El Salvador today or this year?

A. No, I'm not sure of the exact amount.

Q. How many senators have you contacted about your concerns over U.S. involvement in Central America?

A. I have contacted my Vermont representatives.

Q. Have you received responses from them?

A. From [Representative James] Jeffords and [Senator Patrick] Leahy.

Q. Were you satisfied with their responses?

A. Yes. They tended to vote more the way I perceived what was going on down there.

Q. You said before that you were frustrated with the response that you had gotten from Senator Stafford. Is it fair to say that you were frustrated with the fact that he just did not choose to go along with your views?

A. I guess you could say that, yes.

Q. You weren't getting what you wanted, so you became frustrated?

A. Well, I also understood that this war that seems not to be supported by a good number of people in this country according to periodicals like *Time* and *Newsweek* and things like that, it seems to be quite — well, over half of this country is not supporting our involvement.

Q. It's your understanding, Ms. Gaillard, that more than half of this country does not support U.S. involvement in Central America?

A. That's right.

Q. When you were in Senator Stafford's office on March 26th, did you hear Mr. Post and Mr. Pecor ask that everyone in there leave?

A. Yes, I did.

Q. Did you also hear Officer Lawrence and Officer Spaulding ask everyone to leave?

A. Yes, I did. I thought it was kind of strange that my tax dollars went to pay for that office and he was my elected representative.

Q. So you felt then that you could stay there?

A. Well, I understood that an officer was asking me to leave. I assumed that must mean I was breaking the law, but I couldn't really understand how that could be.

Q. Do you think you could have moved in all your belongings as well since you were paying for a part of the office?

A. No. I had no desire to do that.

Q. Were you in the office for the whole weekend?

A. No, I wasn't. I am a farmer and I had to attend to chores.

Q. So is it fair to say that you went back and forth over the course of the weekend?

A. Yes. I was there Friday and I came back Monday.

Q. Did you know on Monday after Mr. Post, Mr. Pecor, Officer Spaulding and Officer Lawrence had spoken, that you were going to be arrested?

A. That's what they told us.

Q. Did you believe them?

A. Yes.

Q. And despite their statements and requests to leave, you still thought you had a legal right to be there?

A. In my heart I felt I did, but obviously I didn't, according to them. They were the ones that had the authority to kick me out of there.

Q. In your mind, did you think you had a right to be there?

A. Yes.

Q. Do you think, Ms. Gaillard, that if Senator Stafford had said, all right, I will hold a public meeting, I will be there in an hour, the strife in Central America would have ceased?

A. Probably not, but maybe his support of the President's funding would have —

Q. Would it have ceased that day?

A. No, but there was a vote coming up soon.

MR. BRADLEY: Thank you, no further questions.

THE COURT: Mr. Nelson?

MR. NELSON: Nothing further, Your Honor.

THE COURT: Thank you very much, ma'am.

JOAN BAUER: Defendants call Janet Shenk.

JANET SHENK, being duly sworn, testified as follows:

Direct Examination by MS. BAUER:

Q. Please state your name and address.

A. My name is Janet Shenk and I live in New York City.

Q. What is your current employment, Ms. Shenk?

A. I am president of the North American Congress on Latin America.

Q. Would you explain to the jury about your organization?

A. It's a research institute founded eighteen years ago that studies the relations between the United States and Latin America.

Q. And what are your current responsibilities with the North American Congress on Latin America?

A. I monitor developments in El Salvador. I travel there frequently as well as carrying out other administrative duties.

Q. What was your previous employment?

A. I have been at the Congress for ten years. Previous to that, I was an economist with the Ministry of Economic Planning in Quito, Ecuador.

Q. So you spent some time in Central or South America?

A. Yes, I have lived there for many years.

Q. And could you please describe to the jury what kind of travels you have done in Central America?

A. I have been to El Salvador seven times since 1982 and I also traveled in Nicaragua, Panama and Honduras.

Q. When were you in El Salvador most recently?

A. Most recently I was there in mid-October, 1984.

Q. And were you in El Salvador any other times during 1984?

A. Yes, I was. I was there for most of January. I was there again at the end of February. I was there in May, June and most recently, October.

Q. And what kind of activities were you engaged in during your travels in El Salvador?

A. Each trip I had a somewhat different purpose. On one trip I was a consultant for a documentary produced for public television. On another trip I accompanied a group of American trade union presidents investigating the situation of trade union rights in El Salvador. Most recently I was there both to cover the recent peace talks and also to monitor the release of some political prisoners in El Salvador.

Q. Did you perform any investigations during any of your travels to El Salvador?

A. Yes, on trips I always conduct interviews with government officials, with human rights monitors, university people, etc.

Q. Have you visited different sites in El Salvador?

A. I have been to, I believe, eleven out of fourteen provinces in El Salvador. I have traveled in many parts of the country, both in zones controlled by the opposition forces and those controlled by the government.

Q. Now, you have also done some writing on El Salvador, haven't you?

A. Yes.

Q. Would you describe for the jury what writings you have done?

A. I am a co-author of a book on El Salvador called *El Salvador: The Face of Revolution.* I have written numerous articles for the magazine published by the institute I work for called *Report on the Americas.* I have written for the *New York Times* and other smaller publications.

Q. Do you also speak the Spanish language?

A. Yes, I am fluent in Spanish.

Q. Now, could you give the jury just a little bit of demographic and geographic information about the country of El Salvador.

A. Well, first it's a very small country. It's about the size of Massachusetts. It has a population of close to five million and it is the most densely populated country in this hemisphere.

Q. We have been hearing today from different witnesses, one of whom testified about political violence in El Salvador. I'd like to ask you, for the jury, to go into a little bit of the history of why people have taken up weapons in El Salvador.

A. First of all I think it's important to note that there was never really a significant armed opposition in El Salvador until about 1980. And what you had throughout the '70s was more a movement of civil disobedience, people took up non-electoral forms of political activity because elections in El Salvador are generally regarded to have been fraudulent throughout the 1950s, '60s and '70s. A watershed year would be 1972 in which, by all accounts, including that of the United States government, the people who won the presidential election in 1972 in El Salvador were not allowed to take office. The army stuffed the ballot boxes, practiced other forms of electoral interference and again, Colonel Arturo Molina was named president in 1972. Throughout the '50s and the '60s, military officers had served as presidents. So, in 1972 you have many people, I would say the majority of people in El Salvador, disillusioned with elections as a way to change the government and get rid of the military as leaders. And so beginning after 1972, you have the first appearance of armed groups but very small and not very significant yet. More significant are the beginnings of mass protest in which the Catholic Church was, I would say, the most important factor in the movement for land reform, for the right to organize unions in the countryside, farm worker unions, for the right to simply lead a more dignified life. So, you have this period which ended with the death of Archbishop Romero in 1980 — that is when he was assassinated. There was a general sense of grief in El Salvador: if they could kill the Archbishop, they could kill anyone and they had been killing hundreds of people. By March of 1980, there was a feeling that more drastic action was needed and then you have the beginning of a very sizeable armed opposition.

Q. And what is the present political climate in El Salvador?

A. It is still a climate of terror in which people are afraid to voice any opinion publicly about what is going on in the country.

Q. And for how long has this type of terror existed?

A. I would say, it's existed since the early 1900s.

Q. Can you give the jury any idea of the dimensions of this terror?

A. Today?

Q. Yes. In other words, can you tell the jury if you know the approximate number of people who have been affected by these various forms of terror?

A. The figure that is generally used in terms of the number of civilian non-combatants that have been killed in El Salvador since 1980 is about fifty thousand people.

Q. In addition to civilians who have been killed, what other forms of terrorism have existed?

A. Fifty thousand are the people that are actually known to be dead. There are also what are called "the disappeared", people who have disappeared from the streets and no one knows their whereabouts. Often they are disappeared by people in uniform. Another category would be people in the prisons of El Salvador, people who have been severely tortured in prison.

Q. Have you visited the prisons of El Salvador?

A. Yes, many times.

Q. Can you describe some of the things that you have witnessed in these prisons?

A. I have seen prisoners whose entire bodies are covered with hydrochloric acid burns. Cigarette hole burns, castrated, I have seen women who have been raped many times. I have seen people with horribly mutilated bodies in prison.

Q. As recently as when?

A. The last time I was in the prison was in May of 1984.

Q. What about other forms of terror, displacement of civilians, is that also going on?

A. There are approximately five hundred thousand displaced persons inside El Salvador and another million living outside the country. Those inside the country are the ones I am most familiar with. They now live in refugee camps, either run by the Catholic Church of El Salvador or by private agencies or by government agencies. These are mainly people, some of whom have lived in refugee camps for the past four years, who had to flee their homes as a result of persecution by the army or more recently as a result of bombings by the air force.

Q. You're leading now to my next question, which is: Do you have an opinion about who it is that is committing these violent acts?

A. I don't think there is much disagreement that the vast majority of the deaths, disappearances, tortures, etc. are committed by elements of El Salvador's armed forces which include both the army and security forces: National Guard, Treasury Police, National Police.

Q. What information are you basing that on?

A. I am basing that on information gathered by both international human rights agencies, human rights groups in El Salvador, primarily the ones connected with the Catholic Church and, in fact, on U.S. government reports that acknowledge that the armed forces are responsible for the majority of the killings. We would differ on the percentages.

Q. What about these death squads we have been hearing about and their relationship to the military? What is that relationship?

A. The death squads in El Salvador are not synonymous, in my opinion, with the armed forces of El Salvador. There are people involved in death squad activity that are not members of the armed forces, and there are members of the armed forces that are not involved in death squad activity. But there is a very significant overlap. According to the best investigative reporting on this subject, the death squads include both retired and off-duty members of the armed forces, but we also see people picked up by heavily-armed men in civilian clothing who later turn up in the hands of the National Police or the Treasury Police or the National Guard. And the government of El Salvador has yet to explain to anyone, to any investigative agency, why these people were picked up by seemingly anonymous agents not in uniform, but later turn up in the hands of official government agencies.

Q. In your opinion, how effectively does the government of El Salvador control these military and paramilitary forces?

A. I think the ability of the civilian president of El Salvador to control the military forces of El Salvador is quite limited.

Q. In this country, we have a military that's controlled by a civilian sector of government. How could such a situation arise as the one we're speaking about where there is a lack of effective control?

A. The military in El Salvador, for fifty years, are used to running the country. They are used to having all the political power. They are used to considerable economic advantage through corruption. And they are used to being able to act with absolute impunity. It is very hard to change that mentality and it is my opinion that it has not changed. The civilian authorities are tolerated by the military because, frankly, they are the ticket to U.S. military aid. I think the Salvadoran army knows very well that if they did not have a civilian president the U.S. Congress would simply not approve military aid.

Q. Now, with these death squads and military acts of terrorism, what kinds of people are likely to be victimized by these activities?

A. I think that the repression today is far more selective than it used to be. So, my answer to your question applied to El Salvador two years ago would have been anyone who was poor.

Q. Why would that be the case?

A. I talked to many army officers and rank and file soldiers who have a perception that the poor of El Salvador have been brainwashed by the press, brainwashed by teachers, all under the influence of some world-wide communist conspiracy, and they would say that very explicitly. So the simple fact of being poor made you suspect.

Q. Would you agree with their assessment?

A. No, I would not.

Q. What is your assessment of the situation?

A. I would say that a major influence on people in El Salvador, who took part in protests or simply who were poor, would be the Catholic Church. The Christian base communities which began in El Salvador in the 1960s were essentially a network of reading sessions, bible study.

Q. And were these groups selected out by the military and the paramilitary for being a particularly suspect group?

A. Priests, nuns, and lay preachers and members of Christian base communities were very much targeted by the military and by death squads to the point where there were flyers handed out in the city saying, "Be a patriot, kill a priest."

Q. What other kinds of organizations were targeted by these terrorist groups and by the military?

A. Any union members. Teachers were particularly suspect. Anyone thought to be an intellectual. Anyone affiliated with the universities. Journalists. There are presently in El Salvador no newspapers that in any way disagree with the government. That is because the newspapers and editors and publishers were either driven out of the country or killed.

Q. These bombing attacks that you mentioned earlier, are they still going on?

A. The bombings, which are conducted by A-37 aircraft, have intensified very, very significantly over the last year. In the month of March, for example, the number of bombings per day was about thirty per day, thirty bombing runs per day.

Q. Where do you get this information?

A. That is information from the Salvadoran military and from human rights monitoring organizations. The bombings have been increasing and account for more and more of the civilian death toll in El Salvador today.

Q. What kind of sites are targeted by the bombers?

A. Areas that are thought by the armed forces to be the sites of guerrilla activity or the sites of populations sympathetic to the guerrillas.

Q. So these are not restricted to military targets?

A. Absolutely not.

Q. What kind of targets? Can you give me some examples?

A. Schools, houses, population centers.

Q. I think it was your statement that that kind of violence has increased in recent months?

A. That is correct.

Q. When you were in El Salvador in January and February of this year, what kind of violence dominated the picture at that time?

A. In addition to the bombing, I would say that army sweeps into zones contested by the guerrillas were another source of heavy civilian casualties. The army enters an area and finds a civilian population; often the guerrillas have already left the area or have never been there. The army, frustrated by not being able to catch the guerrillas, would essentially take out their frustrations on the civilian population, accusing the civilian population of growing crops for guerrillas, of passing information to the guerrillas, of participating in guerrilla-run schools, etc.

Q. Of all these killings you have described, are you aware of the criminal justice system in El Salvador and how it works, and how many of these killers have been brought to justice?

A. I have been told by many, many government officials in El Salvador, army officials and civilian officials, that their judicial system in El Salvador is absolutely non-functional. That was also said to me by the current U.S. Ambassador to El Salvador, Thomas Pickering. No one is arguing that the judicial system functions. To date, no officer in the Salvadoran army has ever been charged with any human rights abuse.

Q. What about these guerrillas and revolutionary forces we have been hearing about? Do they employ the same tactics as the Salvadoran military and paramilitary?

A. There have been cases of abuse of human rights at the hands of guerrillas. Every human rights monitoring agency that I have talked to in El Salvador and the United States agrees that the number of abuses attributed to guerrilla forces is infinitesimal when compared to the abuses by the security forces and armed forces.

Q. You have been in some areas of the country that were controlled by guerrilla forces?

A. Yes.

Q. And what were you able to discern about the relationship between the guerrillas and the civilian population?

A. It varies greatly between different areas. In some areas there was a tremendous relationship between the guerrilla forces and the civilian population. I saw areas in which the teenage youth in towns controlled by the guerrillas were clearly not being recruited into the guerrilla army. They were allowed to continue to go to school, which is not the case in government-controlled zones.

Q. So would it be your opinion then that the same state of terror does not exist in the areas controlled by the revolutionary forces as existed in the areas of control by the government forces?

A. Absolutely. The civilians who are generally targeted are people who are thought to be informers for the government, but they are very few and far between.

Q. Now, the United States supplies military aid to El Salvador, correct? Can you describe what form that military aid takes and what it's used for?

A. The military aid supplied by the United States pays for everything from the bullets and the bombs, the airplanes that drop those bombs, to the airplanes flown by American pilots that tell the Salvadoran pilots where to drop the bombs. It is our reconnaissance flights that provide intelligence to the Salvadoran air force and target the bombing sites. We also pay for U.S. advisors in El Salvador, currently at fifty-five, but actually far higher in terms of officers and U.S. army personnel in El Salvador on temporary duties, which is not included in the fifty-five advisory limit. It is well documented that the American military personnel in El Salvador do far more than just train troops and advise the Salvadoran army. They are present at the highest level of military planning and they are also out in the field advising troops during the battles. I think it's quite accurate to say that the United States is running the war in El Salvador at all levels, in addition to financing the war.

Q. Would that include the war against the civilian population?

A. Very much so. It certainly includes the bombings and also the army operations in the countryside, the sweeps that I spoke of.

Q. Are you familiar with the certification process for the United States military aid?

A. Yes, I am.

Q. Could you explain to the jury what that is?

A. The certification process was the result of actions by the U.S. Congress to oblige the administration, in this case the Reagan administration, to certify that there were significant improvements in human rights situations in El Salvador before releasing any further U.S. military aid to that country. Every six months the President is required to certify to Congress that there is progress being made.

Q. Did the President, in fact, so certify?

A. Yes, he did certify every six months.

Q. And in the years of 1981 to 1983?

A. I believe even until this past July.

Q. Would you agree with those certifications that there were significant improvements in the human rights situation in El Salvador?

A. No, I would not agree with that assessment.

Q. Were there others who did not agree with that assessment?

A. There were many others. Part of the weakness of the certification legislation was that Congress was able to demand this procedure of the President, but Congress had no authority to question or overturn the results of that certification process, so that even if Congress disagreed with the President's assessment, they had no power to deny certification.

Q. Now, there is a statement that some of us have heard from the administration and other sources and the reasoning is something like this: although the government in El Salvador is terrible, the Marxist-Leninist government that might take its place might be worse. Have you ever heard that line of reasoning?

A. Many times.

Q. And do you agree with that line of reasoning?

A. No, I don't. I don't agree that what is at stake or what is being fought for in El Salvador is a Marxist-Leninist government. There are certainly Marxists in the opposition movement in El Salvador. It is a very broad movement. I think it is more influenced by Catholic teachings than by Marx and certainly the concrete proposals set forth by the opposition are proposals that would lead to a very good government in El Salvador. But it would mean that the military can no longer act with impunity in El Salvador and essentially rule the country. The second reason I disagree is that I cannot, based on seven trips there and a great deal of contact with the people, imagine anything worse than what the current state of affairs is in El Salvador, in terms of human rights. There is no free press, there is no freedom of expression, there is no freedom of assembly, and there is terror.

Q. What can we, as United States citizens, do to improve the human rights situation in El Salvador, in your opinion?

A. I think that when the United States government has made it clear to the Salvadoran army and government that we will not tolerate human rights abuses and particularly, when that was coupled with a vote in Congress on military aid, we have seen the death toll drop in El Salvador. The problem is it only drops for a few weeks until the Congress approves aid and then it goes back up again. But it shows that violence on the part of the armed forces can be stopped if there is a will to stop it. I don't think that the U.S. Congress has shown the will to exert real pressure on El Salvador, and I think that what can be done is to exert very strong constituency pressure on our congressional representatives to make sure that our tax dollars do not go for death and destruction in El Salvador.

MS. BAUER: I have nothing further.

THE COURT: Thank you, Ms. Bauer. Ms. Shingler?

Cross-Examination by MS. SHINGLER:

Q. Good afternoon.

A. Good afternoon.

Q. Ms. Shenk, you had mentioned that the President has certified reports every six months regarding human rights situations in Central America and El Salvador in particular. Isn't it true that President Reagan is not alone in his opinion that the human rights situation has improved?

A. I don't expect that he is alone, no.

Q. You mentioned that when financial aid that the United States provides to El Salvador is stopped, that the violence stops; is that correct?

A. No, I did not say that.

Q. What was your statement with regards to the relationship between the violence in El Salvador and the financial aid that is provided by the United States?

A. Financial aid has never been stopped in the last five years. What I said was that when Congress makes it clear that there is a danger of cutting off aid unless human rights are improved, that during the three-, four-, five-week period when the vote is up before Congress, the armed forces of El Salvador go on their best behavior.

Q. But the violence never stops, does it?

A. Completely? No, absolutely not.

MS. SHINGLER: Nothing further.

THE COURT: Ms. Bauer, anything further?

MS. BAUER: I have nothing further.

THE COURT: Very well. Thank you very much, Ms. Shenk.

MS. BAIRD: We call Philippe Bourgois.

PHILIPPE BOURGOIS, being duly sworn, testified as follows:

Direct Examination by MS. BAIRD:

Q. Would you state your name?

A. Philippe Bourgois.

Q. Where do you live?

A. New York City.

Q. What's your occupation?

A. I'm an anthropologist. I'm currently writing my doctoral dissertation at Stanford University.

Q. You're currently working on your Ph.D.?

A. Yes, I am writing my doctoral dissertation on Costa Rica.

Q. Could you explain what that means?

A. Sorry. I'm doing a history of the nationality and racial and cultural history of the population along the Atlantic coast of Costa Rica showing how it changed over the years.

Q. Have you done research in other areas of Central America?

A. Yes, I have been working in Central America ever since college. It's been about eight years now. My honors thesis at Harvard was on Belize. It's a small country in Central America on the coast next to Guatemala. And my Master's thesis was on the Mopan Maya Indians in Belize. I did field work also among the Miskito Indians in Nicaragua.

Q. And would you say that you're fluent in Spanish?

A. Yes.

Q. Did you take a trip to Central America in 1981?

A. Yes, I did. I was looking into the feasibility of doing my doctoral dissertation on Salvadoran refugees in Honduras.

Q. And where did you go at that time?

A. I had been interviewing refugees in the refugee camps in Honduras. These are Salvadorans who crossed over the border into Honduras and sought refuge. I had just begun doing the interviewing when the refugees kept telling me, Look. You keep asking us where we used to grow up. It's only ten miles away. Go ahead, it's right across the river.

Q. For what reason are you interested in these refugees?

A. Well, they are the bulk just in terms of numbers. The largest number of refugees that were accessible in this camp were from that region. As an anthropologist, I decided to focus on that particular area.

Q. You heard testimony before that there are refugee camps in El Salvador. Your testimony is that there are some refugee camps outside of El Salvador; is that true?

A. Yes, I thought it would be safer to do field work among the refugees outside the country, because of the situation in El Salvador today.

Q. What situation?

A. Well, it's very dangerous. There is a civil war going on and a lot of people are getting killed.

Q. What were your interviews, what did they consist of?

A. Well, I was just asking straightforward questions. I was asking the farmers what they grew, what they did when they harvested it, how much rent they paid for their land, how much wage work they did and those kinds of questions. Just the straightforward questions about the mechanics of their life.

Q. Your questions centered on their life in El Salvador?

A. Yes, I was getting history of their particular region to look at what had been happening to them, because I was trying to figure out why there was a civil war going on.

Q. There is a map down here, Mr. Bourgois. Where were you in Honduras?

A. The refugee camps are right here; and this is Honduras. This is El Salvador. This is the border right there. There it is. That's exactly where I was.

Q. Are Honduras and El Salvador friendly governments?

A. They aren't [historically]. They had a war in the '60s but recently that's been changing and as you will see from my testimony the Honduran government actually collaborated with the Salvadoran government.

Q. At this point they are not at war and they are friendly, would you say?

A. Yes.

Q. And they have welcomed refugees into their country?

A. No. Luckily the United Nations High Commission for Refugees has been overseeing the camps in Honduras and trying to ensure the safety of Salvadoran refugees, although there have been cases of kidnaps of Salvadoran refugees in Honduras. It's dangerous for them.

Q. Are there also refugee camps in Nicaragua?

A. Yes, I think every single country in Central America except Guatemala has Salvadoran refugees in it. Belize does. Honduras does. Costa Rica does.

Q. After you did your interviews, what were your findings on the refugee camps in Honduras?

A. Well, it was all very preliminary. I was hoping to do about nine months worth of field work, and I hadn't done even three weeks yet.

Q. And then what did you do after that?

A. Well, I made the mistake of crossing into El Salvador.

Q. Why did you do that?

A. As I was saying, I kept asking them these questions and they kept looking at me and saying, hey, go over there, it's just across the border, it's only ten miles away. And so I did. I crossed over there. I was planning on staying forty-eight hours, just a quick visit to get a feel for the land, to find out if they lived in homestead villages or clustered villages, and so forth.

Q. What was the nature of the border?

A. There is no border crossing there. There is no guard or anything, and there is just a path that the local peasants use and have always used. So I just went across there.

Q. How long did it take you to get over the border?

A. Oh, it took about six hours.

Q. Where did you go in El Salvador?

A. Well, I reached the region exactly below where I pointed on the map, that is known as the province of Cabañas. And I was just going around interviewing small farmers in that region. It's a region of small farmers.

Q. How would you describe that area?

A. Well, it's very typical of any small farming region.

Q. Like Vermont?

A. As a matter of fact, it is a lot like Vermont. It would be like further up north toward the Canadian border, for example. Well, of course, a lot poorer. The basic crops are corn and beans, and the land is owned essentially by a few large landlords, and the bulk of the population sharecrop their land. It's a strange relationship of sharecropping because they have to give a number of days worth of labor to the landlord in return for having access to growing corn and beans which is their subsistence crop.

Q. Could you describe that economic system as feudal?

A. Well, actually, to tell you the truth it's a big debate in anthropology. It's a technical debate about what to call it.

Q. What would you call it?

A. Well, it's certainly a bad deal for the farmer.

Q. Why don't you go on. What do you mean by that?

A. Well, what happens is that the small farmer has to stay in good with the landlord in order to even be given a plot of land to cultivate; and if the landlord just doesn't like him, the landlord won't give him access to any land and he will starve. They're living very close to starvation level. It's not like here. There is no electricity. There is no running water. There are no roads even, and so they're in a desperate situation.

Q. Also no money?

A. Well, money circulates, but they're very short of money.

Q. How about literacy?

A. Oh, about ninety percent illiteracy. Only about ten percent of the population can even read.

Q. Is that area religious?

A. Very religious.

Q. What kind?

A. It's Catholic.

Q. How long were you there?

A. Well, I was planning on staying forty-eight hours.

Q. What happened?

A. At dawn of the day I was supposed to be leaving, the Salvadoran government launched one of its military operations against that region and I was trapped.

Q. Were you expecting that?

A. No, the region had been calm for eight months. There hadn't been a shot fired. As a matter of fact, that's one of the reasons why I thought, well, this area is safe, I will just make a quick trip in and out. And that was my mistake. It wasn't safe.

Q. What happened?

A. Well, it was at dawn and a little boy came running into the hut where I was sleeping. I was staying with a farming family.

Q. Describe the house that you were in.

A. It was shingled. It was a clay shingled house with mud walls and mud floor. It was actually a little better than the typical house there was. Some of them are thatched roofs.

Q. Was there electricity?

A. No, no electricity. No running water. As a matter of fact, there wasn't even an outhouse in this house. And you had to walk about a mile to get to the well.

Q. What happened on this morning that you were talking about?

A. A little boy came running in saying that Salvadoran government troops had surrounded the entire region and that Honduran troops had massed along the river which divides El Salvador from Honduras.

Q. Could you show it?

A. See, this is the river that runs along between the two countries, and Salvadoran government troops had circled this thirty-square-mile region like this, and the Honduran troops had lined up along here; so we were trapped and there was no place we could go.

Q. Why did the Honduran troops do that?

A. They were shooting into the river with the machine guns so that the civilians, the noncombatant regular farming population wouldn't be able to run out and become refugees.

Q. So this young boy told you this?

A. No, he came running in. He was in tears actually saying, "They're coming, they're coming. We're surrounded." I still hadn't quite figured out what was going on.

Q. How do you know who they were?

A. Well, I didn't. I was confused. I had been reading about the region so I knew that there was a civil war going on and I had been interviewing people, but I didn't think it was going to happen to me. And what happened was when the sun got high enough the first helicopter came. It was what they call a Huey helicopter. That's a U.S. helicopter. Everyone in my hut went running out.

Q. Going back to the Huey. It's something that the jurors might not be familiar with.

A. Well, it's actually not too different from the traffic helicopters they use in New York City. It's a big helicopter. They are what were used in Vietnam. It's a standard United States Army helicopter. And they went running out of the hut where I was and I was still standing there trying to let it sink in. They grabbed me and said, Get out of here, we've got to go into hiding. I did. We ran about a hundred yards away, and sure enough when the helicopter got above the hamlet where I was staying, they opened up fire with their machine gun. They were just strafing the entire area with machine-gun fire.

Q. Where were you at this time?

A. We were safe by a clump of trees and boulders and there was a cave that they had dug out of the side of the hill, and so we put ourselves in that cave. I have a picture of it.

Q. When you say "we"?

A. Oh, this was the family. I was with the family that I was staying with. There were several women, and their children.

Q. Were there any soldiers with you?

A. In the region there was armed opposition to the Salvadoran government. Basically these were the young men and young women farmers. They meanwhile had gone down to the periphery of that thirty-square-mile region and they were preventing the Salvadoran government troops from being able to come on foot and kill us.

Q. What did they have as weapons?

A. They had big weapons, formal weapons, and then hunting rifles. Some just had pistols. I'm not really an expert on weapons.

Q. They have any helicopters?

A. No, no.

Q. How old were these soldiers?

A. Basically they were kids. Teenagers. The way I understood it the people with the best eyesight, the fastest runners, healthiest people were the ones carrying the guns because they had very few, and the rest of us — just the normal grandmothers, grandfathers, mothers, children, men and so forth — we were just sort of helpless. The armed opposition had nothing to be able to fire at the helicopters or the airplanes. And the worst was that the Salvadoran government started sending in helicopter after helicopter and airplanes on us dropping bombs on us and then they started lobbing us with mortar fire. They kept this up and we couldn't stand the barrage. At night when the helicopters couldn't circulate and the airplanes weren't flying anymore they would increase the tempo of mortar fire. It seemed like they were doing it indiscriminately throughout the area.

Q. How long?

A. Well, what we would do is, we would be running back and forth from the cave where we were taking refuge when the helicopter and the planes would pass, to the hut where the cooking fire was, to try to eat something. And so we were basically in sort of a state of semi-panic running back and forth trying to find refuge. There were a couple of times when I found myself inside the cave and the cave was full because there were already people inside it. They told me whatever you do, don't panic and run. Stay still, because the helicopter shoots at anything that moves. Motion attracts the eye of the gunner and the gunner opens fire on what is moving.

Q. Did there come a time when you evacuated from that area?

A. Yes, after four days the armed fighters who were protecting us came back to us and said, look, we're running out of ammunition, we're getting desperate. More and more people were getting wounded. Several of us normal civilians had been hit by the mortar fire. They said, you have to get out of here, you have to evacuate.

Q. Going back to the wounded, was there any care for them?

A. No, that was the tragedy. They basically didn't have any real medical care.

Q. Any pain killers?

A. There were no pain killers. There was a little boy — I will never be able to forget — had a mortar scrap in his legs and they just held his feet and pulled out the mortar scrap. He later died. We buried him along —

Q. When it came time to evacuate, what happened?

A. We assembled together. There were about a thousand of us regular, normal small farmers.

Q. You have some pictures of people you were with?

A. Yes. It was grandmothers, grandfathers. There was a blind woman with us. There were several pregnant women. Many babies and two women actually gave birth during the flight. I have a picture of one of the women just after she gave birth.

Q. Mr. Bourgois, I'd like to show you what has been marked Defendants' C through J for identification. Could you tell the Court what those are?

A. Yes, these are pictures, all but three of them, that I took during the military invasion. I had a little camera with me.

Q. When did you take these photographs?

A. I took them during the whole military operation as it was happening.

Q. And you took these yourself?

A. Yes.

Q. Are they accurate representations of the people you were with on this trip?

A. Yes.

Q. How long was that military operation?

A. We were all under fire for fourteen days before we finally made it out as refugees.

Q. And those are the originals of those pictures?

A. These are, yes, and these are color photo xeroxes of the slides.

Q. I would like to offer these into admission.

THE COURT: Very well.

Mr. Bradley?

MR. BRADLEY: Your Honor, if I may take a look at them?

THE COURT: Of course.

Voir Dire Examination by MR. BRADLEY:

Q. While I'm doing that, Mr. Bourgois, I believe you stated before that all except three were taken by you?

A. Yes.

Q. Do you know offhand which three were not?

A. Yes, there were three that were taken by NBC News. NBC News was filming us as we became refugees in Honduras, and it was the *Today Show*. And these two were taken by *Today Show* photographers as we were crossing the river. And this one, this woman crossing from El Salvador into Honduras is also taken by the *Today Show*.

Q. Where did you get those particular photographs from?

A. From *Today Show* photographers.

MR. BRADLEY: Your Honor, State would have no objection to the introduction of the photographs taken by Mr. Bourgois. However, we would object to the photographs taken by a yet unidentified photographer from NBC. And also on the bottom of some of the photographs there is some writing, and I think before that should be admitted there should at least be some further explanation of that by Mr. Bourgois.

MS. BAIRD: Your Honor, if I may respond. I believe that Mr. Bourgois has testified that this is a fair and accurate representation of the people that he was with. I don't believe that the rule requires that the photographer who took the pictures be available here today, and I would ask the Court to admit all of them. And I will gladly provide an explanation through Mr. Bourgois for the writing that appears on these pictures.

THE COURT: Very well. With regard to the NBC News photographs, sir, were you present in that general area?

A. Yes, actually that's why we made it out alive. They had come down to the border area where the Honduran soldiers had been, and that's what forced the Honduran soldiers out of the border area and allowed us to pass. They didn't want to get caught on U.S. television shooting civilians; that's how the coast was clear for us to make it out alive as refugees.

THE COURT: And these folks in these pictures were some of the people that were with you and are known to you?

A. Yes.

THE COURT: And these photographs are fair and accurate, too?

A. Yes.

THE COURT: Very well. Defendants' C through J, inclusive, are admitted; and the comments written on the bottom of the photographs are not to be considered by the jury absent an explanation by the witness. They may be marked.

Defendants' C through J were admitted at this time.

Direct Examination continued by MS. BAIRD:

Q. These pictures portray people you were with? What kind of people were they?

A. Well, these are the people, these are the farmers that lived in this region. These are just the local inhabitants of this area.

Q. And there were women as well as men?

A. Yes, people of all ages and all farmers, as a matter of fact.

Q. What happened after you evacuated that region?

A. We had a hard time evacuating. There were about a thousand of us, and we were filing single file trying to sneak out of the area and go into hiding. And the hope was that the fighters, the people protecting us, the boys, were going to do a diversionary tactic and get the Salvadoran government troops to attack them. They were going to make a lot of noise, shoot their guns off to our left and we were going to run out as fast as we could on the right and hopefully go into hiding. What happened, though, is when we got right to that line of fire, the babies that the mothers were carrying started to shriek and cry because of the fright of the gunfire. And at that point the Salvadoran government troops changed the direction of their machine-gun fire and started shooting into the sound of crying babies. Now, at that point it was pandemonium, grenades were landing on us. Machine gun fire was coming on us. We were hitting the dirt, getting up and running as fast as we can, and the babies shrieking, and the fire getting stronger and stronger.

Q. And women carrying the babies?

A. Yes, you see the mother has to carry her own baby, because if a stranger picks up the baby, someone the baby isn't familiar with, the baby shrieks even louder. So the mother is the only person that can try to quiet her baby. That was our biggest risk.

Q. Why was that?

A. Because Salvadoran government troops — well, it appeared that they wanted to just do away with all forms of life in this region, and the sound of screaming babies was attracting their machine fire.

Q. Did you somehow escape?

A. Yes. I was running at one point and a grenade went off about from me to where the jury is and I hit the ground and the mud and the rocks are flying all over. I got on to my feet and was running forward and there was a little boy, the grenade had landed on him and taken off his legs — I'm sorry, it's a horrible story to tell — had taken off his legs and that was my first immediate contact with that, and I stood up and grabbed my head and I was saying what do I do, carry him? He was not dead yet, and I was sort of trying to figure out what was going on when someone came up behind me, pushed me hard so I fell down and then I heard, "Keep running, you're in the line of fire. You can't do anything for him," and I kept on running.

Q. Where did you run to?

A. Well, about three quarters of us, about six, seven hundred of us managed to run out into a ravine a few miles away. And when dawn was breaking, we found ourselves huddled into the ravine. They were patrolling up above us looking for us, and thank God they didn't find us.

Q. Did you stay in the region very long?

A. Basically for the next eight days we ran at night and we hid during the day. You see, we had to run at night, because at night the helicopters couldn't circulate and the helicopters were the big risk for finding us.

Q. Did you go to the Honduran border?

A. No, we wanted to become refugees. It's logical for civilians to become refugees in a state of war like that, but we couldn't because of Honduran troops lined along the rivers. So we actually had to flee away from the border during that first period. We were just zig-zagging and trying to make sure that the government troops' foot patrols wouldn't catch up, and each night we would have a different place or, as much as we could, a better place to hide and we had no food.

Q. Or water?

A. Well, we had a hard time with the water. There were streams we drank out of, but since there were so many of us and many people were wounded by this time we kept contaminating the water. As a matter of fact, that was one of the reasons we had to move.

Q. Did there come a time when you went back into that region?

A. Yes, after eight days of this flight we thought it was over, and we started to file back into the region we fled out of, and the first thing that hit us as we were walking back was the stench of rotting meat, because what the Salvadoran troops had done is they had killed every living creature that they had been able to get their hands on. They were even killing the cats and the dogs, the pets. They had tried to rip down the houses. They had ripped apart the granaries. The granaries seem to be the first thing that they went for, and they actually tried to stop the harvest. It was a period of bean harvest which is a very important harvest for Salvadorans, and they had zapped that, and that's what we walked into.

Now, what happened was a Salvadoran battalion which is trained by the United States participated in this invasion, and they were using what they called the new Green Beret-style, Vietnam-style tactics of leaving behind small groups of armed men to do ambushes after you finish the basic invasion. We didn't realize this, and the next thing we knew we were ambushed and again they surrounded us. For another two days we were submitted to the mortar fire, to the fire by the Huey helicopters and to bombardment by the airplanes.

Q. Did you see many deaths during that time?

A. I didn't during those last days, I didn't see any more deaths. No other people were blown up next to me, but by that time we had a serious number of wounded people and trying to care for them was a big problem. Our other big problem was the babies, because the mothers' milk by this time was drying up because of the lack of food, and the dehydration from terror. And the babies were crying a lot, and that was dangerous for us because once again it gave away our exact position to the patrols.

Q. Eventually what happened?

A. Well, what happened was, an NBC film crew had gone just by luck to the Salvadoran refugee camps and they were doing a regular public story about refugees and the situation of refugees. While they were there, they heard this bombing and strafing and so they said, well, let's see what is going on; and they walked down to the border which was only about five miles away. And that's what forced the Honduran troops to get out of that border area and cleared it so we civilians could come out into safety; and that's what we did. As soon as we found out the path was clear to the refugee camps we just ran. It was an all night run for me. I made it out just as dawn was breaking. Most of the people were mothers carrying their children. They went much slower. And they were hit once again. Daylight caught them when they were still in El Salvador, and they were hit once again with the strafing by the helicopters. And they didn't get out until later that afternoon and some even until the next day.

Q. How many days did this go on?

A. It was fourteen days.

Q. You ended up in a refugee camp again in Honduras?

A. Yes.

Q. Perhaps you could show the jury the pictures of the people you were with on that trip.

The witness distributed the pictures.

A. This is the family that I was staying with. This is the very first day I was in the cave. This is the cave. The helicopter just passed and we were waiting to see if it was safe.

This is a picture of a crater that one of the bombs made. This is a horrible, horrible picture. It is not the mother. That's a young baby, the father, and his two-year old son. The mother was blown up as we were running through the line of fire by a grenade. Miracle the baby wasn't killed. But there was no one to feed the baby, and I thought she had died. But I went back to the refugee camps in Honduras a year ago and she was alive. Not well, but she was alive. This is taken by the NBC photographers just as we made it over into Honduras, and we had an incredible feeling of momentary relief.

This is us crossing over the river in Honduras. Here we are crossing. And this is a woman with her three children. She was barefoot. I don't know if she made it out alive, because I didn't see her at the refugee camp. She had given me cookies. That was the second day. I realized later that we were going to be out of food, and I shouldn't have taken her cookies.

This is us hiding during the day. As you can see, one of the things that gave us sustenance was sugar cane. We were running through some sugar cane fields. We would cut them and bring it with us and distribute it at night. This is a woman. She just gave birth to this baby. Second night of the flight she gave birth to the baby. When I went back to the refugee camp I saw her alive and well.

This was a little boy that I made friends with. This is that very first dawn that we fled out of the region, and we were hiding in that ravine. See, we're all scrunched up together. The helicopter had just passed looking for us, so we were down like that.

Q. Mr. Bourgois, did you learn while you were in that area who the guerrillas were?

A. It came as a shock to me actually. One of the things I thought I was going to be looking at was the relationship between what we call the guerrillas and the local population. And what came as a shock was that the guerrillas were the kids who ran the fastest and had the best eyesight and so they had the guns. There was a limited number of guns, and the rest of the population was their grandmothers, their grandfathers, fathers, their wives, their daughters and their children.

Q. And the government then is just attacking these civilians, these villages; is that what you observed?

A. Yes. This is the tragic logic of what's called in the press, "counter-insurgency warfare." When you have a situation like that, where the large majority of the population is opposed to its government, and the government won't accept any kind of public criticism, the government just kills you if you oppose it. The logic is that you have to kill everyone because the grandmother is going to make beans for her grandson, and her grandson is the one carrying the gun. They just want to kill everyone in these regions; kill every living creature.

Q. Before you went to this area, did you have a political opinion about it?

A. Well, I'm an academic. And I try to read everything I can on Central

America.

Q. Have you read everything you could?

A. Well, you never read enough, but I was familiar with the literature of all spectrums. And I had an idea of what was going on. See, as an academic you try to be objective as best you can.

Q. When you came back to the United States, did you attempt to inform your government about the findings that you had made in El Salvador, about the nature of the war and about what had happened to you?

A. Yes, I did.

Q. What happened?

A. Well, I had a hard time. Initially the NBC film crew interviewed me on their television camera. We were in terrible shape. We were emaciated. We hadn't been eating. We were bloody. We were traumatized, and they broke down in tears and said this is just terrible. They said, "Quick, come back with us tomorrow; we're going to take you to our editors. We're going to announce this to the American public. They should know about this." So we did that. We went back to New York and they called up their editors and their editors said they didn't want me on the show. They had enough and it wasn't dramatic enough. Then I went to the *New York Times* and I talked with the senior editor and showed him my pictures. He listened to me and he said, "Well, we have had a lot of guerrilla stories. We don't need any more." Then I went all over the place. I went down to Congress, and I visited, one by one, all the senators in Congress who would see me. I went to the State Department as well. I couldn't get it out. It was very upsetting. It took me six weeks before the National Public Radio and Associated Press finally did a story.

Q. And you subsequently have had articles in the press?

A. Subsequently I was on the *Phil Donahue Show*, and I testified in Congress.

Q. Were there any attempts to discredit your testimony?

A. Yes, the United States Central Intelligence Agency did an investigation of me. I only found out about this because their investigation, I'm proud to say, backfired. It turned out that I wasn't a bad guy. They presented to a group of congressmen an analysis of me saying I was propagandizing and basically calling me a liar. And what happened was the Congressional Committee to whom they presented that report wrote up another report saying this is an example of an exaggeration by the Central Intelligence Agency. We, too, have done an analysis of this young man and he is fine and he has a right to share his opinion.

Q. One final question: In your flight from El Salvador, were the people you were with mainly noncombatant or combatant?

A. We were all noncombatant. The way it works is the people with guns keep as far away from us as possible. They always stayed about a mile or so away from us. And they would prevent the government troops from being able to come in on foot and kill us. And whenever a government patrol, for example, would get too close to us they would attack it and then run off and try to draw the fire on them and take it away from us. So we were the noncombatants.

Q. Have you been back to Honduras to the refugee camps?

A. Yes, I went back.

Q. And do you have some art from those camps?

A. Yes, I do. I asked the school children to draw pictures. The question was: Draw pictures of where you grew up. And they drew really upsetting pictures. They had all been through these kinds of military operations. Some had been through the very same one that I went through. These military operations are continuously happening.

Q. When did you collect those pictures?

A. These were collected in the summer of 1983.

Q. As an anthropologist, Mr. Bourgois, are those the common tools of your trade, the art of people?

A. Well, this is the kind of thing that one can look at to try to get a feeling for the psychology of the population. In a sense children never lie in their drawings. And what is frightening about these pictures is the consistency of them. They are all showing horror scenes of war.

MS. BAIRD: Thank you very much.

Cross-Examination by MR. BRADLEY:

Q. Mr. Bourgois, you said that when you came back from your trip to El Salvador and Honduras that you went to the American Congress in Washington, and while you were there you spoke with a number of congressmen and senators. Do you recall how many of the congressmen and the senators you managed to speak with?

A. Well, I usually ended up speaking with their aides because it's hard to get access to the congressmen themselves. I contacted roughly twenty-five or thirty congressmen and senators. I actually spoke with four or five. In March of 1982, I testified before the House Subcommittee on Inter-American Affairs on Human Rights.

Q. And when you were speaking with the actual senators and congressmen, what was their response to your experiences?

A. Well, there was one particular case which was gratifying. He grabbed his head when I told him the story; he grabbed his head in his hands and said, "We'll have to live through the Vietnam experience again!"

Q. Who was that? Do you recall?

A. You know, it's terrible, I don't remember.

Q. What other responses from congressmen or their aides?

A. They all listened to me.

Q. Is it fair to say that some more than others?

A. Oh, certainly, yes.

Q. Did any try to explain to you what their feelings and reasonings were?

A. Well, you see, I only got to talk to about three or four of the congressmen. The aides don't really talk, they're not presenting their opinions.

Q. When you testified was it before the whole Congress?

A. No, it was before the House Subcommittee on Inter-American Affairs. Actually, what happened was that none of the Republicans came to the event.

Q. Were you invited to testify at that?

A. Yes, I was.

MR. BRADLEY: Okay, thank you. I have no other questions.

THE COURT: Ms. Baird, anything further?

MS. BAIRD: No further questions.

THE COURT: Very well. Thank you very much, sir. I appreciate your coming down.

At this time we're going to recess. I'd like to mention again that you folks should avoid any news articles or radio broadcasts or television broadcasts. I mentioned that last night and I think perhaps it might be helpful if I just indicated why that is. I'm sure you're probably aware of why, but the reason for it is that you're going to have to decide the case just on the testimony here in court and the news articles are not necessarily accurate. Indeed, I did happen to see one item during the past day which was flat inaccurate with regard to this particular matter. It does happen, and we want to guard against that. Also, it's not fair to the parties because they don't have a chance, like they do here in court, to visit with the people who are reporting events to us. And also, you don't get a chance to see the demeanor of the people who are reporting. So those are the reasons for it, and so I would again ask and urge your cooperation on that. It is important and there are good reasons for it. It's not just some legal rule.

We'll start tomorrow morning at nine o'clock, and I hope you folks have a good evening and I appreciate your being with us today. Thank you.

Court adjourned for the day.

Open court, November 15, 1984, nine a.m.

THE COURT: Next witness.

OLIN McGILL: We'd like to call Shaila Sherwin.

SHAILA SHERWIN, having been duly sworn to tell the truth, the whole truth and nothing but the truth, testified as follows:

Direct Examination by MR. McGILL:

Q. Good morning.

A. Good morning.

Q. Would you please tell us your name.

A. Shaila Sherwin.

Q. Where do you live, Shaila?

A. I live on Long Island in New York.

Q. And what do you do there?

A. I am a student at Friends World College. I work with the Salvadoran refugee community on Long Island.

Q. Where is Friends World College located?

A. There's a location on Long Island in Huntington, but as well it's an international program with centers on every continent throughout the world; in Central America, Asia and Africa, etc.

Q. Have you studied in any of those foreign countries?

A. I went to Costa Rica in January of 1983 to begin my Latin American studies.

Q. Can you tell us what you do working with the refugees on Long Island?

A. On Long Island I work with the Central America Refugees Committee. We're in the process of organizing a health clinic for the Central American community. The community itself does not have access to the health care needs that very often are required. Access is limited due to the fact that they are very fearful of seeking such medical assistance because they're considered undocumented.

Q. How many refugees are there in the Long Island area?

A. In the Long Island area there are twenty thousand, although it does not appear that there are twenty thousand because you would very rarely come across a Salvadoran refugee in the street.

Q. How many are there in the New York metropolitan area?

A. In the New York metropolitan area there's a total of forty to forty-five thousand, although it's important to note it's very difficult to come up with figures because of the fact that they're undocumented.

Q. Do you know how many refugees outside the country of El Salvador there are?

A. Out of a population of five million, there are one million living out of their country in Canada, Honduras, Guatemala, Mexico, and throughout many other countries.

Q. So one out of five Salvadorans is living outside Salvador?

A. That's correct.

Q. How did you begin to work with the Salvadoran refugees?

A. When I went to Costa Rica to begin my studies in Spanish and Latin American history, one of my professors of the Friends World College was a Salvadoran living in exile in Costa Rica. Through a friendship that I began to develop with her I learned of such things as her son being killed and her house being bombed, and other things that I never imagined. It had a great deal of impact on me. From there, I was introduced to the Salvadoran community and I began to be really concerned about what was happening to them and finding out more about why it was happening to them.

Q. Did you ever work in a refugee camp?

A. In Costa Rica my studies were focused on just kind of understanding the experience of the Salvadoran refugees. After traveling, visiting other Salvadoran communities in other countries in Central America, such as Nicaragua and El Salvador, I decided to go to Honduras and work in a refugee camp. And that was the first time I actually lived and worked with the refugee community.

Q. When did you go to the refugee camp in Honduras?

A. That was November of 1983.

Q. How long were you there?

A. A total of eight months, which means I left in June of this year.

Q. Could you come down to the map and indicate on the map where your camp was?

A. See right over here, it was three miles from the border of El Salvador, which means the refugees had come across walking; and from the camp you can see Salvadoran territory and any refugee could point out which town is which and which direction they had come from. And although the border is very unclear because it's a very mountainous region, the refugees themselves knew where the towns were located.

Q. What was the primary focus of your work in the refugee camps?

A. What had the greatest impact on me was the effect on the children of their experience in El Salvador, in their travels to get to the refugee camps, and their experiences in their refugee camp. And the total of these experiences had a major impact on the children, and that was to me the most important focus of my work there.

Q. You've got with you some pictures which you took; is that correct?

A. That is correct.

At this point, a number of documents, including photographs, leaflets, and children's drawings, were examined by the prosecution and admitted as evidence.

Q. Can you explain to the jury what these pictures are about?

A. Well, just to give a general idea of the life in the camps, we start with this picture which depicts a woman and her daughter making tortillas over a wood oven. That is their basic diet: tortillas, rice, beans, and coffee, which come from the United Nations and the other international agencies that are assisting the refugees. This is a picture of an elderly woman sitting in a nutrition center which the refugees themselves have developed to help provide more nutrition to the elderly, the malnourished, the young infants, and the pregnant women. Over a long period of time, from what I observed, their diet of rice, beans, and tortillas causes the refugees to develop a deficiency of vitamins and minerals, although it's very rich in protein. You see, the children, who are fifty percent of the population in these camps, are much older than they appeared to be. The development of their physical bodies, to my understanding, was due to their diet. They appeared much younger than they actually were. Compared to the children here in the U.S., they looked three or four years younger than they actually were.

Q. Were they smaller?

A. They were smaller, shorter; and most of them had very large stomachs, as you see with these two young sisters.

Q. What are the children like? Are they well behaved?

A. The children are very well disciplined. Rarely, actually never, did I see a parent discipline a child in the sense of yelling at them, or hitting them, or any kind of discipline like that. The children play among themselves, although, as you could see here, they have very few toys or anything to play with. This young boy is playing a musical instrument, a cello, which they made in the camps out of some plywood.

Part of my job was to work with the children in the workshops. The workshops are a network of thirty-six shops which produce necessities for the camps, such as shoes, clothing, hammocks and things like that. Because fifty percent of the population are children, they were very important to the work force.

Here there is a group of young children learning to embroider and to sew. This was very important for the children in that it was preparing them for their future and they were meeting the needs of the camps. I have here two pictures on the education that is happening in the camps. I had the opportunity to help to capacitate the teachers who had arrived from El Salvador. Many of them were unable to read and write and now, through the international agencies and international workers, they are beginning to learn to read and write. They are then able to teach their children or other adults who did not have the opportunity to learn. The illiteracy rate of the camps was eighty percent in 1981, and after four years it has dropped to forty percent.

You see in this picture a helicopter flying over the camps, and there's a group of children, at the bottom, with school notebooks in their hands. Being on the border zone, as I pointed out on the map, there is a great deal of military activity and there is a constant movement of planes and helicopters.

Q. You said there's a lot of military activity there. Could you identify marks on the planes or helicopters?

A. We couldn't identify the marks on the planes because they were flying very high.

Q. Did you ever see signs of bombs?

A. Here is a picture of a jet. It was a very common occurrence to see what they call an A-37 jet bomber sweeping down in this fashion, and you could see the actual bomb dropping from the plane and within a few seconds you could hear the explosion and actually feel the earth tremble.

Q. Were those explosions in El Salvador or Honduras?

A. These were in El Salvador.

Q. Was there ever any military activity in the refugee camps?

A. Well, the Honduran military would very often patrol the area of the camps, often passing right through the camps. The effect of this would be that when the soldiers would enter the camp, I would see the children running inside their tents and they would break out into hysterics and they would cry. This came from their knowing what that means, having seen the soldiers in El Salvador.

Q. And while you were working with the children did you ever see them draw pictures of their experiences and life in El Salvador?

A. Many of the children were not very communicative. The medium in which I was able to most understand the impact of their experiences was through their drawings, and I brought with me some of those drawings.

Q. Have you ever studied art?

A. I have studied the psychology of art for the past three years. Some of the program was psychology of art, and some was psychology.

Q. Can you describe what the psychology of art field is about?

A. Well, basically it's interpreting the psychology of the artists through their artwork. Specifically, with the refugee drawings, it's the interpretation of the artwork as an indication of the state of mind and the psychological well-being of the children.

Q. Based on your study of psychology and the psychology of art, do you believe that you can draw conclusions about the impact on the children of what they have been through by looking at the art they draw?

A. Yes, I believe it's a very accurate medium in which children are able to communicate, in a very simple way, experiences they're often not able to communicate with words.

Q. Why aren't they able to communicate with words?

A. Their experiences, their youthfulness, and their fearfulness can cause them to repress a great deal. My experience has been that most of them refuse to talk about what they have seen, whereas they can draw what they have seen.

Q. Could you show the drawings to the jury and describe them?

A. Well, I'll show this drawing and give an explanation, and the rest I will just submit. This drawing here depicts a variety of things. The green men are the soldiers because it's labeled *la guardia*, which means the guard. This up here, see the burning of people here, and this soldier is saying: "We're killing guerrillas," and this soldier is shooting at a woman and a little girl lying on the ground that's yelling "Mama, mama." And the soldier is saying "Yes, we're now killing you." And there's a group of children hiding over here that are saying: "Oh, we hope to God that they're not going to kill us." And there you see a woman hanging from the tree with a rope around her neck, another child here, a beheaded person here, and a helicopter shooting on this house and it's burning up into the air. Most of these drawings are similar in that they have beheaded people and dismembered parts of the body, and pregnant women being shot at, and helicopters or airplanes flying down.

Q. What can you conclude about the children's state of mind from pictures like these?

A. From pictures like these, the details that can be observed of the soldier, of all the belts and the cartridges, and the detail of the gun, indicates that the child has a real recollection. It's not from her imagination or his imagination because of the detail, of the accuracy of the helicopter, of the soldier. It has had an impact on the child to the extent that it can be reproduced at any moment into a drawing such as this, where bodies are dismembered and bugs are eating the dead bodies.

Q. Anything hopeful in these pictures?

A. Well, after seeing those kinds of drawings, I asked the children to make another drawing of how they hope El Salvador would be.

Q. This was a specific question that you asked the children?

A. Yes. How they would see El Salvador in the future. And in the future of El Salvador there are farmers and people going to school, and children playing. And the explanation written by their teacher says: "All we want is to work in our farms, and to go to school, and to have a life of being able to work in peace."

Q. Thank you. No further questions.

THE COURT: Very well. Thank you. Mr. Bradley?

MR. BRADLEY: No questions, Your Honor.

JENNIFER STRICKLER-VENCEREMOS, having been duly sworn by the Court to tell the truth, the whole truth and nothing but the truth, testified as follows:

Direct Examination by MR. McGILL:

Q. Could you state your name?

A. My name is Jennifer Strickler.

Q. And Ms. Strickler, are you a Defendant in this case?

A. Yes, I am.

Q. Where do you live?

A. I live in South Burlington.

Q. And what do you do for a living?

A. I'm a Research Assistant at the University of Vermont.

Q. What are your duties there?

A. I design and analyze data from different surveys on student life at UVM.

Q. Ms. Strickler, do you speak Spanish?

A. Yes, I speak Spanish fluently.

Q. Did you study Spanish at the University?

A. No, I studied Spanish when I took a trip to Guatemala, and I studied Spanish in high school.

Q. Did your study in Spanish lead you to take a trip to Central America?

A. Yes. In the summer of 1983 I spent three and a half months traveling in Central America to learn Spanish.

Q. Your main interest then in going to Central America was not particularly political, but to learn Spanish?

A. Yes, I knew very little about Central America before I went.

Q. Did you go to Guatemala?

A. I spent three weeks in Guatemala studying Spanish. I traveled in Honduras and Nicaragua, and Costa Rica, and El Salvador. And I also spent some time in Panama and Colombia, which are not part of Central America.

Q. What did you do there? Did you speak to the people?

A. I traveled and spoke to everybody that I could since I was trying to improve my Spanish. And I went to movies. I went to the beach. I participated in regular life with the people in Central America.

Q. Can you describe these countries? Can you describe the similarities between them?

A. Well, they all speak Spanish, and they're all mainly agricultural countries that are very poor. The per capita income is under one thousand dollars in all of those countries. That's how much money people earn a year. They're all predominantly Catholic, and they all have a strong military presence.

Q. All of those countries have soldiers that are obvious in the population?

A. Yes, soldiers travel. Everywhere you go you see soldiers. Some of them have machine guns. I don't know much about armaments, but they all carry some kind of arms. You see them everywhere you go, on the buses, and in the streets, and in the parks.

Q. Are there differences in the reactions of the people to the military of their countries?

A. Yes, there were very noticeable differences.

Q. Can you describe them?

A. Well, the main thing that I remember is that in El Salvador, which people have talked about a lot, and also in Honduras and Guatemala, the people are terrified of the military forces.

Q. How do you know that, Ms. Strickler?

A. Well, when a soldier gets on a bus or comes into a park or comes into a restaurant, or just appears any place, then there's silence. Everybody is quiet and they watch the soldiers to see what they're going to do, and they try and get their kids to be quiet. And the kids huddle by their mothers' skirts, and there's a real sense of fear. You can feel it in your heart when a soldier comes into a place. Whereas in Nicaragua it is very different. The soldiers there were seen more like we see our policemen here, that they are people that you go to when you have a problem. And they're a resource for the community, for people that have a problem, like a lost kid.

Just to clarify, I know this is really confusing, Nicaragua is the country that the United States does not give any kind of military aid to. In fact, we give military aid to the forces that are trying to overthrow the government.

Q. Those are the contras?

A. Those are the contras. Another thing about Nicaragua that I noticed: it was the only country where there was any kind of opposition to the government. They had an opposition press that was able to print editorials or articles, or things that were not a hundred percent in favor of the government, or the army. In the other countries there was no opposition press at all.

Q. Did you read the opposition press?

A. I read every newspaper I could get my hands on.

Q. In all of the countries?

A. In all of the countries.

Q. *La Prensa* is the opposition newspaper in Nicaragua?

A. Yes.

Q. Is it circulated freely?

A. Yes, just like the other newspapers.

Q. Is it expensive or cheap?

A. It's the same price. The paper boys and paper girls go around with all three newspapers, including *La Prensa.* It's just like any other newspaper.

Q. Did you read the newspapers in El Salvador, Honduras, and Guatemala?

A. I didn't get to read the newspapers in El Salvador but in the other countries I did.

Q. Did you notice that there was an opposition press there?

A. No, there was no opposition press.

Q. Is there a difference, in your view, between Nicaragua and the other countries, in the amount that people are able to criticize their government?

A. Definitely. In the three countries that are supported by the United States, people are unwilling to be the least bit critical. A lot of people were afraid to talk to me just because I was an American. They were afraid to talk about their government. They were afraid to talk about our military aid to their government. They said it's very dangerous; there are ears everywhere. I heard that constantly, that there are ears. And in Nicaragua that wasn't true. For the most part, the people strongly support their government, but they also told me that there were problems in the land reform. The peasants wanted land, and that wasn't being done as quickly as they wanted. And there was no fear to express opposition to their government. They knew they wouldn't be killed, whereas in the other countries the chances are that if you say something against the government, you'd be put on a list and you'd be targeted to be killed.

Q. In Nicaragua specifically, did you see any signs of war there?

A. Yes, I saw signs of war everywhere. I spent one night near the border of Nicaragua and Honduras, which is where the contras — the counter-revolutionary forces — mainly live and I heard a barrage of gunfire like there was a battle going on. And also, the people in Nicaragua told me constantly that they needed to defend themselves, that they were being attacked.

Q. Did the people in Nicaragua know who was attacking them?

A. Yes, they did. They knew that the contras were coming from Honduras and that they included people that used to live in Nicaragua and left because they opposed the government, and that they also included people from other countries.

Q. Ms. Strickler, did your trip to Central America affect your political views?

A. Yes, it did. Before I went, I was unaware of the political turmoil that was going on down there. I knew that there was some kind of war, but I didn't know anything about it. Since I got back from my trip, I've read everything that I can about the region, and I'm really concerned about what is going on and about the role that the United States is playing.

Q. What kind of things did you read?

A. I read the *New York Times*. I read several books on Central America, including the book that Janet Shenk, the woman that testified yesterday, wrote. And articles in *Time* and *Newsweek* and other kinds of periodicals.

Q. Did you become politically active on your return from Central America?

A. Well, one of the things that I did was try to contact my congresspeople to tell them about my experiences. Within two weeks of getting back, I wrote to Senator Stafford and Senator Leahy to tell them about a bad experience that I had in Honduras.

Q. Was that at the border?

A. That's right. When I was crossing the border into Honduras, the border police took away a book that I had gotten in Nicaragua. They said that it was illegal to carry material from Nicaragua into Honduras. And they also strip-searched me. They made me take off all of my clothes, and they put — I'm sorry.

Q. They searched your body?

A. Yes.

Q. And you wrote your senators about this, and what was the response?

A. Senator Leahy sent me a letter thanking me for telling him about this, and that I should keep in touch with him about Central America. I received no response from Senator Stafford.

Q. How many times did you write to Senator Stafford with your concerns?

A. Well, that was the one time that I wrote to him. After that I called his office twice asking that he send me a position paper on Central America, and that he meet publicly with people to discuss Central American issues. From my interaction with Congressional representatives, I knew that Senator Leahy and Congressman Jeffords were both concerned about Central America. Senator Stafford was not; it was not his area of interest.

Q. Did he communicate that?

A. Through his aides he communicated that. I also visited his office twice; once in January and once in March. About two weeks before we all went to his office, I made another visit and talked to his aides, Rey Post and Peg Bowers. They said that he did not have a position paper on Central America and that it would not be possible for us to meet with him because his schedule was booked up.

Q. And did you express the idea to them that you have expertise on Central America, that perhaps he should meet with you?

A. I could understand that he didn't know anything about it because he's very busy, but I felt that it was really important for him to get this information. I know that several other Defendants have traveled in Central America and a lot of us have spent time learning about it. I thought that it was important for us to convey that information to him.

Q. Was it that sense that led you to the demonstration in Winooski last March?

A. Yes. That's what was in my mind. We had information that I thought was crucial to get to him because there were votes coming up in Congress and he's an influential Republican senator. If we could change his mind, that would influence other Republican senators as well.

Q. Did you go to the demonstration with the idea of having a public meeting with him?

A. That's right.

Q. Throughout that weekend did you feel that you had lawful authority to be there?

A. Absolutely. I thought that I had information that was crucial to give to Senator Stafford, and that it was my right and my duty as one of his constituents to give him any information that might help him in forming his foreign policy votes.

Q. Thank you very much.

THE COURT: Thank you, Ms. Strickler. Mr. Bradley?

Cross-Examination by MR. BRADLEY:

Q. Good morning, Ms. Strickler.

A. Good morning.

Q. I have just a few questions. Ms. Strickler, what was the name that you gave the law enforcement officers when you were arrested on March 26th?

A. Jennifer Strickler-Venceremos.

Q. Venceremos was not the name that you gave today; is that correct?

A. That's right.

Q. Is Venceremos a name that you were born with?

A. No, it's not.

Q. Is it a name that you have obtained through marriage?

A. No, it's a name that I added to my name. It means in Spanish, "We will overcome;" and it was an expression of my beliefs.

Q. So your name in translation is, Jennifer Strickler-We-Will-Overcome?

A. Yes.

Q. Ms. Strickler-Venceremos, were you not aware of the fact that Senator Stafford had agreed to meet with some representatives of your group on Monday, March 26th?

A. He was not willing to meet with us on Monday, March 26th. He said on March 26th that he would meet with a group of representatives from the people that were visiting his office, and I did not consider that satisfactory. I thought that he had an obligation to meet with all of his constituents that were concerned, just as Senator Leahy and Congressman Jeffords had already done.

Q. So at the time you were arrested you were aware of the fact that he had agreed to some sort of meeting with members of your group; is that correct?

A. That's correct.

Q. Now, isn't it true that your demand to Senator Stafford was for a public meeting?

A. Yes.

Q. Now, if Senator Stafford had dropped everything and flown up from Washington and convened a public meeting on Monday, March 26th, do you really believe that the fighting and the civil war would have stopped at that time in Central America?

A. I think it would have been a crucial first step; there was a vote coming up and he is an influential member.

Q. So you're saying yes, that if he had had a public meeting the fighting would have stopped on March 26th?

A. No, it would not have stopped on March 26th; it would have been a first step.

MR. BRADLEY: Thank you.

THE COURT: Thank you.

Mr. Nelson, next witness.

MR. NELSON: Defense calls David A. Rosenberg.

DAVID A. ROSENBERG, having been duly sworn by the Court Officer to tell the truth, the whole truth and nothing but the truth, testified as follows:

Direct Examination by MR. NELSON:

Q. Would you state your name, sir, and give your address?

A. My name is David Rosenberg. I live in Middlebury, Vermont.

Q. Your current position, Mr. Rosenberg?

A. I am an Associate Professor of Political Science at Middlebury College.

Q. Would you tell the jury something of your academic background?

A. I was trained first at the University of Pennsylvania, where I received a Bachelor of Science degree in Economics; a Master's degree in International Development from Cornell University; a Ph.D. in Comparative Government in Southeast Asia from Cornell University. I have been a visiting professor at the University of the Phillipines, at the Johns Hopkins School for Advanced International Studies; and at Cornell University Center for International Studies. Those are my formal training and official positions.

Q. What was the specific field in which you concentrated in your studies?

A. I have studied primarily Third World politics and U.S. foreign policy toward the Third World. I have been very interested in the issues of insurgency. I have done a lot of work on Vietnam, on the Philippines, and more recently on Central America. I have also done consulting for various government agencies, and a few other non-governmental agencies.

Q. Do you consider yourself an expert in United States foreign policy, specifically applied to Central America?

A. Well, yes, I guess I do; although in many ways I still feel as if there is a lot more to know about that part of the world. I haven't done as much field work there as I have in other places, such as Southeast Asia, but certainly with regard to U.S. foreign policy, I would regard myself as well-informed.

Q. During this past year, Mr. Rosenberg, you were on leave from Middlebury; is that correct?

A. That's right. I was a visiting professor at Johns Hopkins School for Advanced International Studies. I was also a visiting lecturer at the Foreign Service Institute of the State Department. Both are in Washington.

Q. And did you do any consulting work?

A. Yes, I did a lot of consulting last year, primarily on the Philippines after the assassination of [Benigno] Aquino. It became a major public policy concern for the United States government which has many, many interests there. I consulted with the State Department Bureau of Intelligence and Research, the State Department policy-making staff, the Foreign Research Institute, and Congress. I consulted with the House Foreign Affairs Committee, the Senate Intelligence Committee, the Defense Department, the Defense Intelligence Agency, the CIA, and the Office of Global Affairs and Issues. I think those are the major ones.

Q. Sounds like you spend a lot of time in the corridors of power.

A. Yes, but I live in Vermont.

Q. In your work in Washington, did you come to learn anything about the current United States policy in Central America?

A. Yes, I did, very much so. Primarily from people I had been previously working with on issues related to Vietnam and the Phillipines. I discovered that increasingly they were working on Central American affairs. That was the period of the big buildup of covert operations in Central America and many of the people I had associated with previously were now in Honduras or else working on Central American matters. That's how I first learned that something really big was going on that was not widely known in this country.

Q. So a number of your prior contacts had been assigned to Central America?

A. That's right, and in particular they were concerned with trying to coordinate an increasing number of activities in different countries and in the United States.

Q. Let me ask you this: did many of these people share a common past in government?

A. Share a common past in government? Well, several of them were colleagues working on issues of insurgency, counter-insurgency, and the formulation of U.S. foreign policy in various countries. They had that much in common.

Q. Where were they assigned in the '60s and '70s?

A. Well, mostly in Indochina and especially in Vietnam, which is where I came to know them first.

Q. So the same folks who were involved in government policy in Vietnam have been reassigned to Central America?

A. Yes. These are people who are not the top political appointees, but the administrators specializing in counter-insurgency, insurgency, intelligence analysis, and covert operations. They have now become more general or all-purpose crisis managers, and go from place to place trying to coordinate activities in the field and in the different agencies.

Q. From your contact with these people and others in government, what did you learn about United States policy in Central America?

A. Well, by the time I arrived in Washington, things had been going on for a while. There was already a covert war going on, sponsored by the U.S., to try to destabilize or remove the Sandinista government in Nicaragua. It had been going on since December, 1981, when the National Security Council first approved the plan for covert operations.

Q. What forms did this strategy of destabilization, as you call it, take? What specifically did the United States do?

A. It did many things. Probably the first thing that happened was an economic blockade, an economic boycott. The U.S. cut all economic aid to Nicaragua. It cut its sugar quota. It asked its allies to cut their economic aid, to stop buying sugar from Nicaragua. It started lobbying the international agencies, the World Bank, and other commercial banks, to stop lending credit to Nicaragua. That was probably the first response, an economic one. The covert operations took a little longer to organize, to staff, to pull together. By the time I arrived in Washington last August, I was surprised to discover that there were already about five or seven thousand so-called contras, sometimes called "freedom fighters", that the U.S. was pulling together, mostly in Honduras — equipping them, training them, doing some joint operations with them — primarily under CIA direction. And that was the first major need for coordination back in Washington: to find all these people from various countries, to pull them together, and to supply them. It was a joint venture between the CIA and the Special Operations Forces of the Defense Department.

Q. So in your view, the CIA and other branches of the U.S. government are actually organizing and sponsoring the contras?

A. Yes. They have been for about three and a half years now. And it has become somewhat bigger. By the time I arrived in Washington, not only was there a large force of contras in Honduras, but the CIA was already beginning to escalate their acts of intervention: air strikes, mining of the harbors and ports of Nicaragua, and direct military actions, primarily carried out by the contras on the ground, but with a lot of CIA support from aerial bombardment and naval vessels.

Q. Where did the contras get their weapons?

A. From the CIA.

Q. What sort of weapons do they have, do you know?

A. They have a wide variety of weapons, mostly small arms. Increasingly, they have fairly standard-issue weapons available widely throughout the region because the U.S. has greatly increased its military aid to the Honduran government and the Salvadoran government, as well as the contras.

Q. You mentioned mining of the harbors. What other sorts of tactics do the contras use?

A. Raids over the border, against villages, were started back in March, 1982. That's over two and a half years ago. Then they started escalating the following year. The main oil refinery was attacked at least twice and there were several strikes against other fuel storage depots. Several hospitals, schools, and bridges were hit. I think probably bridges have been the single most popular target for the contras. I don't have a current estimate of the death and destruction that's resulted from this; I'd guess probably about three or four thousand fatalities, plus many more injuries.

Q. Is this the civilian toll you're talking about, or military toll?

A. These are civilians. There have not been too many direct contacts between the Sandinista forces and the contras. It's really been a hit-and-run type of low-level warfare.

Q. Why hospitals and schools?

A. I think these have become major sources of support for the Sandinista government. The Sandinistas came to power in late '79 and started a program of building schools and rural health clinics which were very popular, and as a result the contras targeted them to try to undercut the popular support for the government.

Q. Moving from the contras for a moment, has there been any direct United States troop involvement in the region?

A. Yes there has, primarily in the form of air and sea forces, and to a limited extent some ground combat forces, and also a lot of trainers and special operations forces with the CIA. The Big Pine Operations in 1983, I think, involved perhaps the most U.S. forces, about thirty thousand. That was a military exercise off both the Atlantic and Pacific coasts of Nicaragua.

Q. Perhaps you could step down for a moment, Mr. Rosenberg, to the map here and show us the locations of the United States naval and land operations.

A. The U.S. has two main naval battlegrounds; one over here on the Caribbean side, and the other on the Pacific side. There are about one hundred fifty ships in all. Some of them have planes on board. There are also about seven different airfields, two major ones and five minor ones. Most of them were built in the past three years. There are, of course, other back-up bases just a few flying hours away, mostly in Key West, Florida, which is a U.S. naval air base. It has just been reopened to support U.S. forces in this region. And the central command for all U.S. forces in all of these countries is Special Operations, Fort Bragg, North Carolina.

Q. Thank you. You can resume your seat. How many U.S. troops, total, have been involved in the region in the last few years?

A. Total, well, there were thirty thousand in Big Pine Two, and about fifteen thousand in Big Pine One. There was an earlier ocean exercise, I think it was called Ocean Float Exercise, which had about fifty thousand. There are about one hundred fifty CIA agents in Honduras. There are about one thousand U.S. combat advisors and trainers in Honduras. There are others in Guatemala and El Salvador, which I haven't counted in these totals.

Q. What, in your view, is the purpose of all these military exercises?

A. There are several purposes. With regard to Nicaragua, I think the main purpose of the current administration is to remove the Sandinista government from power in Nicaragua through a variety of means: some covert actions, some intimidations, some economic, some psychological, and if necessary, as a contingency I imagine, with U.S. combat forces.

Q. Did you, in your career in Washington, gather information about the future course of U.S. government conduct towards Nicaragua?

A. Yes. The future course is to steadily increase the pressure on all fronts, covert, overt, economic, psychological, unless there is some significant U.S. domestic opposition. I think there are two major oppositions. The first is, I believe, that the Joint Chiefs of Staff will be very reluctant to commit any large number of U.S. combat forces on the ground in Nicaragua, unless it is widely supported in Congress and in the country. And this is certainly not the case in Congress. Congress has repeatedly tried to stop the covert war.

Unfortunately, Congress has not had all the information I believe they should have to play the role they're supposed to play in foreign policy-making. A lot of this is due to less than complete candor by the CIA and Defense Department with the Congressional Committees that are supposed to be governing these affairs.

Q. Did you hear anything about the possibility of plans for a hot war, an overt U.S. invasion by U.S. troops?

A. Yes, there have been two. Last year the most complete preparation for possible intervention was the so-called Pegasus Plan, which involved a combination of the contras and U.S. combat support forces from naval and air bases. It was originally described as an exercise, but they went through all the motions of an invasion, including landing one thousand U.S. Marines in Honduras. Ultimately they did nothing, primarily because of Congressional opposition. It was scheduled to happen in May. One month earlier, in April, there was a big leak about the mining of Nicaraguan harbors. That caused a very strong reaction in the U.S. Congress, which immediately voted to censure the CIA and started to cut funding for any military intervention and passed a resolution in Congress declaring that no U.S. combat forces should be introduced to destabilize the Nicaraguan government. That resolution was passed in Congress last year and had the very successful effect of heading off the Pegasus Plan.

Q. So, there is some opposition in Congress to intervention; is that correct?

A. Yes. In particular to the covert war, including the mining, the air strikes, the ground attacks. I think there's been significant opposition ever since the secret war operations were discovered. In November, 1982, some very nervous caseworkers inside the CIA leaked out the information about this escalating covert war, and that led to the Boland Amendment. Representative Boland of Massachusetts got a bill passed to cut off all funds from the U.S. government to the contras, and that temporarily stopped the secret war. But the administration came back the next year, in March of 1983, to Congress and asked for fifty million dollars to continue the covert war. On the whole, the Senate went for it and the House didn't, and as a result they came up with a compromise which left twenty million dollars for covert action in Nicaragua. Then the mining started.

Q. Who paid for these mines?

A. The U.S. taxpayer.

Q. Through what agency were the funds funneled?

A. Through the CIA.

Q. If the concerned citizen was interested in trying to stop these goings on, what door should he or she knock on?

A. I have personally knocked on the door of the member of the Senate Intelligence Committee who's from Vermont, Senator Leahy. I think any senator, any representative, and in particular, those on the authorized Oversight Committee, should be informed of what is going on. All too often they have complained that they don't know anything about what they're supposed to be supervising until they read about it in the newspapers. This is what happened with the minings. This is what happened with the air strikes. Senator Leahy has been on public record, saying they were supposed to be informed about all these things, but were not. The most recent example of this kind of end run or camouflage of covert action by U.S. government agencies has been the preparation of the counter-insurgency manuals for the contras. The Congressional Review Committee didn't know about it. They didn't know the CIA prepared manuals which included plans for the assassination of Nicaraguan government officials.

Q. So basically, in returning to my question, you knock on a door of some elected representative?

A. Yes.

Q. You characterize the United States policy as one of trying to destabilize the government. Is there another justification that's given out for what the United States does?

A. There have been a few. The original justification given for covert action against the Nicaraguan government was that the Nicaraguan government was supplying weapons and other support to the rebels in El Salvador. This was the charge. This was the justification used when the administration went to Congress and asked for fifty million dollars for covert action against the Sandinista government. However, there has been very little evidence, in my view at least, of Nicaraguan government support for rebels in El Salvador. At least for the past three and a half years there has been no evidence presented by the administration to support the justification. That leads me and many others to question whether the U.S. is interested in stopping the arms flow from Nicaragua to Salvadoran rebels, or whether they really want to get rid of the Sandinista government. I think the clincher about this particular point came with the revelations about the CIA training manuals for Nicaraguan counter-revolutionary forces, the contras. There is no mention in those secret training manuals of arms interdiction. The whole focus of the training manual is insurgency.

Q. Very briefly, Mr. Rosenberg, could you tell us what the CIA is telling the contras to do in these manuals?

A. I certainly can. I have seen them before in Vietnam, and before that in the Philippines, where the first drafts were written by virtually the same people. The same text now appears in these counter-revolution manuals. They describe methods of disturbing the economy, of economic warfare, sugar in gas tanks and things like that. They talk about how to use terror and violence selectively, how to identify strategic leaders to neutralize or assassinate. I think many of the manuals have now been published in this country.

MR. NELSON: I have no further questions.

THE COURT: Mr. Bradley?

Cross-Examination by MR. BRADLEY:

Q. Professor Rosenberg, I believe you said it was about two years ago that fifty million dollars was requested by the present administration to carry on covert activities in Central America.

A. Right.

Q. And that the American Congress, after negotiations, denied the administration that fifty million dollars; is that correct?

A. No, not exactly. Every spring the administration sends its request to Congress. There was a very big debate, especially in the light of previous disclosures about the secret war. Strong sentiments were expressed in the House to cut off aid to the war by the U.S. against the Sandinista government. In this particular case the controversy went on all through the summer and fall and it wasn't until late November, 1983, that there was finally a compromise reached in the Conference Committee. The Senate agreed to cut all aid for covert operations. The House agreed to support a lesser amount of money. About twenty million dollars was finally authorized in November, 1983.

Q. And was that compromise then voted on and passed, by Congress and the Senate?

A. It was.

Q. How long did the debate go on between the time the administration requested the aid and the time it passed?

A. On and off for about three months when Congress was in session. This is not the first debate they've had on covert operations. It started a year earlier and still goes on.

Q. It's fair to say, then, that there is quite a difference of opinion in the halls of power in Washington over United States' involvement in Central America?

A. Yes.

Q. You mentioned at one point that you feel there has been less than complete candor on the part of the CIA and the present administration?

A. Right.

Q. Is that your opinion?

A. Oh, no, it's not my opinion. I think this is the opinion of every outraged member of Congress, of the Senate Foreign Relations Committee, and the Intelligence Committee, who should have been informed that the money they voted for was going to be used for such things as mining. They didn't know about the mining. They didn't know about the air strikes.

Q. When you made that statement, though, were you speaking for them or were you speaking for yourself?

A. Well, I am not sure there's a difference, actually.

Q. Is it your opinion that there has been less than complete candor —

A. Yes.

Q. — on behalf of the CIA and the present administration?

A. That's correct.

Q. And is there a feeling in Washington that there is, however, candor on behalf of the administration, and the CIA?

A. No, I don't think so. I think the CIA, in particular, has felt that if they asked for funds for mining or for air strikes, they would be denied; and therefore, they have gone ahead and done them without telling Congress.

Q. So everyone in Washington, then, believes that the CIA is being completely truthful?

A. No, I didn't say that. Let me repeat it again. The CIA and the Defense Department got together in what is now a well-organized joint special operations agency. They have not disclosed what they know to be the policies and plans which would meet objection in Congress. And they have done that presumably to continue their funding. Their funding was cut off three times. It's a battle over what U.S. foreign policy should be, and I think that's quite legitimate. If somehow the Nicaraguan government does constitute such a serious threat to American security that it justifies potential military intervention, then surely it ought to be discussed openly and completely in Congress and in the nation. That's the objectionable part of the CIA and Defense Department actions; they were trying to pull a fast one over on Congress in particular, and perhaps the rest of the country as well.

Q. And is that the opinion of everyone in Washington, all of the senators and all of the congressmen?

A. No, it is not the opinion of everyone. There is a lot of opposition to the covert action. There is also a lot of support for it.

Q. Thank you.

MR. BRADLEY: No other questions, Your Honor.

THE COURT: Thank you, Mr. Bradley. Mr. Nelson?

Re-Direct Examination by MR. NELSON:

Q. You were asked about support for this operation. Are you knowledgeable at all, Mr. Rosenberg, in the field of International Law?

A. Knowledgeable, yes. I don't teach that subject.

Q. Could you give it a try?

A. I will try.

Q. To your knowledge, the acts which are committed by the United States government, directly or through the contras; do they constitute violations of international law?

A. Yes, a few laws. The economic boycott and embargo are a violation of several international agreements. It's a violation of the General Agreements on Tariffs and Trade that govern trade among nations. It's a violation of the International Law of Contracts. The case was argued by the government of Nicaragua in the International Court of Justice. The U.S. government did not contest that case, and the International Court of Justice voted for the Nicaraguan government. The U.S. disregarded it.

Q. How about organizing the contras' funding for their activities in Nicaragua?

A. I believe that's a violation of U.S. law as well as international law.

MR. NELSON: No further questions, Your Honor.

THE COURT: Mr. Bradley?

MR. BRADLEY: No questions, Your Honor.

THE COURT: Very well. Professor Rosenberg, the H-37 Huey used in the area, where does it come from?

MR. ROSENBERG: Which H-37 Huey are you referring to?

THE COURT: I think that was the designation. There has been some testimony about jet fighter bombers used in that area.

MR. ROSENBERG: I don't think they're being used in Nicaragua. I think they're a part of the air force of Honduras, and Guatemala, and to a lesser extent, El Salvador. There are U.S. forces with that equipment also there. Not all of the helicopters and other battle planes are for those other governments. They're also for U.S. bases in those countries.

THE COURT: Very well. Mr. Nelson, Mr. Bradley; anything further? Mr. Nelson?

MR. NELSON: Just one question.

Re-Direct Examination continued by MR. NELSON:

Q. These planes and helicopters, who manufactures them?

A. I am not exactly sure who manufactures them.

Q. Country, in what country?

A. They're American, mostly manufactured by the United States. The U.S. has very large military programs.

Q. How did they find their way to Central American airfields?

A. How do they get there? I think they just fly them down. The United States government has a very active military aid, military training, military sales program to Honduras, Guatemala and El Salvador; several hundred million dollars of it now. And that has increased considerably in the past years, since the Sandinista government came to power in Nicaragua. I think it's part of the general U.S. plan of arming anti-Sandinista forces to try to pressure the Sandinista government out of power.

MR. NELSON: Thanks.

THE COURT: Mr. Bradley?

Re-Cross-Examination by MR. BRADLEY:

Q. Professor Rosenberg, does the United States government also supply planes, military equipment to the Sandinista government?

A. It used to.

Q. Does it not any longer?

A. It doesn't anymore.

Q. Who does? Where do they get their equipment from?

A. They have purchased equipment from a variety of countries. They don't have very much in the way of planes, perhaps less than a hundred various aircraft, none of them long-range or none of them regarded by our government as aggressive. The planes they have now are from France, from Czechoslovakia, from — I would have to check my sources to see what other places.

Q. Do you know if they have purchased Soviet-manufactured [planes]?

A. No, I don't think they have any Soviet planes.

Q. Do they have any other Soviet military equipment?

A. Yes, they have Soviet tanks. They have a lot of American small arms, rifles.

Q. So is it fair to say that the government will buy military equipment from just about anybody that will sell it to them?

A. What they can afford, yes.

MR. BRADLEY: No other questions, Your Honor.

THE COURT: Mr. Nelson?

MR. NELSON: Nothing further, Your Honor.

THE COURT: Thank you very much, Professor Rosenberg.

LEA TERHUNE, being affirmed to tell the truth, the whole truth and nothing but the truth, testified as follows:

Direct Examination by MR. NELSON:

Q. State your name and address, please.

A. My name is Lea Terhune. I live in Colchester, Vermont.

Q. Are you a Defendant in this case?

A. Yes, I am, sir.

Q. And are you employed?

A. Yes, I am.

Q. What is your employment?

A. I work as the Executive Director of Vermont Dental Care Programs.

Q. How did you come to be interested in Central America?

A. I traveled in the country of Nicaragua in February of 1984, just prior to my son turning eighteen years old, at which time he would have become eligible for the draft.

Q. What kind of traveling did you do in that country?

A. I traveled to the northern border region to the village of Jalapa, where contras had been attacking the villages of the area.

Q. Who did you travel with?

A. I traveled with a group of people with Witness for Peace.

Q. Could you explain to the jury what that group of people is and what it does?

A. Witness for Peace is an organization that sprang from a trip that a man by the name of Henri Nouwen made to that same area. He observed that the attacks and the killing of the village population stopped when Americans were in the area. He got the idea that if American citizens would be willing to be there day after day, that we could effectively stop the killing there, and it worked. Vermont was the seventh state to put together a group of people to go as part of Witness for Peace.

Q. How many people were in your delegation?

A. There were twenty of us.

Q. And what did you do when you were in Nicaragua?

A. I traveled to the border village of Jalapa, and spent approximately a week there, constantly interviewing people, and taking photographs. We traveled north of the village to the border area, where there was another small village. We could see Honduras on three sides. We talked with people whose children had been killed, whose churches and schools and health care centers had been attacked by the contras, and got eyewitness accounts from the individuals in the village.

Q. Could you describe the political climate in Nicaragua, based on your experience there?

A. The political climate was very tense. It felt different in the border area where there were attacks and the war was imminent. The rest of the time I was in Nicaragua I spent in Managua, interviewing church people and government officials. And there the tenseness wasn't as immediately personal as your children getting killed. It was more a political tenseness. They felt and believed that an attack by the United States was going to happen any minute, and everyone was trying to defend themselves and protect themselves.

Q. What kind of actions did you observe in that regard?

A. Well, I observed people on Sunday out in the backyard digging bomb shelters. Typically they built them behind houses and near the area where the women would be hanging up clothes and the children would be playing.

Q. What impressed you the most in your trip to Nicaragua?

A. I think the thing that surprised me the most was when I was in Managua and had the opportunity to meet with representatives from the nine opposition parties to the Sandinistas. We met with individuals and representatives of churches and human rights organizations and local community groups and there was constant love and support for the Sandinista government and the Sandinista army. I thought when I met with the opposition parties, the political opposition, that finally I was going to hear someone speak against the Nicaraguan government, as indeed I did. They had many complaints about the Nicaraguan government.

The thing that surprised me was that I thought I'd finally found a group of people in Nicaragua who supported the activity of the contras. I asked them directly; I said: "Do you support the activity of the contras against the Sandinista government?" And they all looked at me, shocked, like they hadn't heard me right. And they said: "No, absolutely not. No, we don't. There can't be political dialogue and open educational process when a war is going on." And that surprised me a great deal. Nowhere, at any time in the country did I find anyone who supported the contras, or who had anything but fear for what the United States was doing.

Q. How do you feel you were received in Nicaragua, personally?

A. I was personally received very warmly, with an incredible amount of love and hope from the people, and that was hard to understand until some young people explained to me that they had experienced life in Nicaragua under Somoza, who was a brutal dictator. The Somoza family ruled the country with an iron fist for over fifty years. The people had experienced this, and they understood that people are different from their government, and they could accept me as a person from the United States who wasn't doing the things to them that our government is doing.

Ms. Terhune then spoke at some length, under questioning, of her efforts to educate and influence Senator Stafford about Central America.

MS. BAUER: No further questions.

THE COURT: Thank you, Ms. Bauer. Ms. Shingler?

Cross-Examination by MS. SHINGLER:

Q. Good morning. You have described your activities with Witness for Peace on direct testimony. Is it my understanding that the purpose, or one of the purposes for Witness for Peace is to actually stop some of the tragedy and killing in Central America?

A. Yes, that's right.

Q. And that was the purpose for you going down to Central America with Witness for Peace?

A. That was one of my purposes, yes.

Q. Focusing on that particular purpose, do you feel that you were successful in decreasing, in any way, the tragedy in Central America by your visit with Witness for Peace?

A. Yes, I do.

Q. You actually feel you stopped some of the killing by being there?

A. When I traveled on roads that had been attacked by the contras, and held the hands of the children riding on that truck with me, I knew and they knew that they were safer because an American citizen was by their side. They knew that the contras would not dare to hurt them with a Witness there.

Q. So, you felt that there were direct and immediate results and changes because of your presence in Central America; is that true?

A. For the people that I was with in that village during the time that I was there, it brought them hope. I protected them, and it brought me information and eyewitness information that I could bring back to this country because we weren't getting very much good information here.

Q. Wouldn't it be fair to say that your trip with Witness for Peace was more successful in stopping the tragedy in Central America than your activities on March 26th?

A. No, I don't feel that way.

Q. Do you know whether or not you prevented any of the tragedies by sitting in Senator Stafford's office?

A. I do not know that for sure.

Q. But you have a very strong feeling?

A. I have a strong feeling about both activities, that both of them helped to protect the people in Central America.

Q. But you know that your trip to Central America actually made somebody more safe; is that correct?

A. Certainly didn't make me more safe.

Q. You have just testified on cross-examination —

A. Your question is confusing me, I'm sorry. I feel strongly that my presence in the village of Jalapa, and my presence in Senator Stafford's office, equally helped to protect the people in Nicaragua who are in danger.

Q. Two ways of protecting?

A. That's right; one by being there in person, and the other by petitions to the Senator upon my return.

MS. SHINGLER: Thank you.

THE COURT: Ms. Bauer?

Re-Direct Examination by MS. BAUER:

Q. When you came back from Nicaragua, did circumstances permit you to go back down to Nicaragua immediately and continue the types of activities that you had done there?

A. No, they did not. I used my vacation time to go there and I have very little of it.

Q. Thank you.

MS. BAUER: I have no further questions.

THE COURT: Thank you. Ms. Shingler?

MS. SHINGLER: Nothing further, Your Honor.

THE COURT: Very well. Thank you very much, ma'am. We'll take our noon recess at this time and resume at one-thirty.

Noon recess was taken. Open court.

THE COURT: Next witness?

LINDA VANCE: We call David MacMichael.

DAVID MacMICHAEL, being duly sworn to tell the truth, the whole truth and nothing but the truth, testified as follows:

Direct Examination by MS. VANCE:

Q. Would you state your name and address please?

A. My name is David MacMichael, and I reside in Weston, Virginia.

Q. Mr. MacMichael, what is your occupation?

A. At the present time I'm a consultant. I deal with political and economic development, usually in the foreign relations area.

Q. Could you tell us a bit more about your work; give us an example of the sort of work you do?

A. Yes, for example, one of my clients who is representing a group with interest in the country of Colombia, South America, asked me to do a brief study on the possibility of political instability or violence within that country, and I provided them with that information.

Q. Could you tell us something about the education and work experience that's prepared you to do this type of job?

A. Yes. I am trained in history and I hold a Doctor of Philosophy degree from the University of Oregon with a specialization in the history of the United States foreign policy. I taught Latin American history for some years. I was a United States Marine for ten years, resigning as Captain in 1959. I worked for about a dozen years for a major research institution, the Stanford Research Institute, now known as SRI International, in Menlo Park, California. I have performed a number of studies for the Defense Department and other agencies, both in Latin America and Southeast Asia.

Q. What did you do from 1965 to 1969?

A. 1965 through 1969, I was a Senior Social Scientist with SRI International, and performed studies on insurgency and counter-insurgency in South America, and in Southeast Asia.

Q. What did you do between 1981 and 1983?

A. From March of 1981 to April of 1983, I was an Estimates Officer with the National Intelligence Council, which is the senior staff of the Central Intelligence Agency, responsible for coordinating the work of all the foreign intelligence agencies of the United States government.

Q. Were you working as a policy consultant when you performed functions as an Estimates Officer for them?

A. No, I was not a consultant in the sense of being an outside contractor. I was fully integrated into the Central Intelligence Agency with complete security clearance and complete access to intelligence, having passed through all the standard clearances and lie detector tests and so forth.

Q. Was there any raw intelligence material that you did not have access to?

A. In the areas with which I dealt there was no intelligence to which I could not have access, no.

Q. Thank you. While you were working for the CIA were you asked to study the different characteristics of what I would call the insurgency movements in El Salvador and Nicaragua?

A. Well, obviously one of the reasons I was hired by the agency was because of my background in the field of insurgency and counter-insurgency and part of my duties was the preparation of estimates relating to the insurgency in Central America. I was called upon to give my expert opinion on the characteristics of them, yes.

Q. I wonder if you could give us a brief definition of the term "insurgency"?

A. Insurgency refers to an armed movement directed against an established government, for the purpose of overthrowing that government. It differs technically from a revolution in the sense that it typically does not involve a widespread breakdown of that civilian government in the first place; but instead it's a persistent armed movement, usually based in a political movement designed to overthrow a well-established and well-seated government.

Q. What is the difference between the nature of the anti-government movement in El Salvador and the anti-government movement in Nicaragua?

A. Well, I will give this as an opinion, but I will hope you will treat it as an expert opinion. The movement in El Salvador is an indigenous movement which took long years of political preparation, within the country, to create a mass support base within the civilian population. It is the result of many years of a viciously oppressive military-controlled government and it finally came into its present form of existence after a series of fraudulent elections accompanied by a great deal of state terror during the mid and late 1970s.

The movement is an indigenous one. It has purely Salvadoran leadership which comes from across the Salvadoran political spectrum. It relies largely on an internal support supply base. I say largely, because the movement does get support and material assistance from outside the country from a wide variety of sources. The emphasis here, though, is on the fact that it has required a long, painful political preparation within the country.

In contrast, the so-called contra war which is going on now in Nicaragua is basically what one might call a counter-revolution. You can't export revolution simply because it requires such a long political preparation within a country, while in the case of counter-revolution where a previous government has been overthrown through insurgency or other means, the former structure is still largely in place even though damaged, so it is very easy to export counter-revolution as is now occurring in Nicaragua. The remnants of the former National Guard fled into Honduras. With the former political and economic structures it's been a relatively easy matter for outside forces to arm, train, and direct these so-called contras.

The counter-revolutionaries operate entirely from outside bases in Honduras and Costa Rica against the existing government of Nicaragua. So there is a considerable difference between the two movements.

Q. You say that there are outside sources supporting and organizing the contras.

Who are those outside sources?

A. Basically, the contras have been organized, directed, and led by the United States government.

Q. Are there any mercenaries within the ranks of the contras?

A. Mercenaries is a difficult term to use there. There are certainly people who have been recruited into the ranks of the contras on the promise of high pay which has been provided largely by the United States government. There are certainly people who fly aircraft on dangerous missions for the contras into Nicaragua, who by anyone's definition, are mercenaries. There are professionals who do this for pay, yes. This is my very strong belief.

Q. When you were working for the CIA, was anything brought to your attention as a reason or justification for the United States supporting the contras?

A. Well, the reason brought forward originally was for the United States to support a limited operation designed to stop and interdict an alleged arms flow going from Nicaragua to the FMLN insurgency in El Salvador.

Q. Have you ever seen any evidence that there is such an arms flow?

A. The government of Nicaragua, together with many other governments, both within the Central American region and outside it, were, from November 1980 until no later than April of 1981, engaged in the business of transporting arms to the FMLN. This is admitted by everyone. At the end of that period the new administration which had taken over the government of the United States in January of 1980, said severe consequences were likely to follow if the Nicaraguan government did not cease abetting the transfer of arms into El Salvador. And after that there is essentially no evidence of any Nicaraguan government involvement in the transfer of arms into El Salvador. Such evidence as exists is very, very scanty, and in most cases, of less than complete reliability in my judgment.

Q. Did you, in working for the CIA, attempt to find evidence of such an arms flow?

A. Oh, yes, I did. As I mentioned earlier, my background for some years has been in counter-insurgency matters, and I had my academic background in Central America and Latin America; and so it was not surprising I found myself working on this subject. When the contra war became a fact and was being justified on the grounds of an arms flow, I was a bit alarmed; first of all, because of the very scanty evidence; and second, because I did not see it. Indeed, there had not been any prior analysis of the quantity of arms, what types of arms they were, what routes were being used, what means were being used for delivery, what the support system for receiving those arms within El Salvador was, what the storage and distribution means of those arms within El Salvador were: all sorts of things that one would have to know if one were to mount a successful effort to disrupt an arms supply system. Another glaring omission, in my judgment, was that no attention was being paid at all to alternative sources of arms from the outside to the insurgents. So, simply from a professional point of view I busied myself in calling up the intelligence available on the arms flow to try to make some determination as to where the arms were coming from and in what quantities. In my judgment, there was no substantial evidence of a continuing flow of arms from Nicaragua into El Salvador.

Q. Mr. MacMichael, at the time that you were searching unsuccessfully for evidence of an arms flow, was the United States administration continuing to allege that the reason for supporting the contras was that very arms flow?

A. Oh, yes. There were public statements by the administration, by the United States Ambassador to the United Nations, statements of the Department of State, statements of the Department of Defense, that continually justified support for the contras for the sole purpose of stopping the arms flow. As you know, when the controversy over the support of contras reached public notice and our so-called covert war became a very overt one, in the debates in Congress over continuing appropriations to support the contras, the only justification advanced by the administration was that it was needed to interdict this arms flow. As a matter of fact, the so-called Boland Amendment, which was adopted by both Houses of Congress, prohibited appropriations of any funds for the contras except for the purpose of interdicting this arms flow. And there was no arms flow.

Q. Mr. MacMichael, in your opinion, if indeed the arms flow was not the reason for the U.S. support of the contras, what was the real purpose of the United States giving such aid and support?

A. Oh, I believe that the real reason has been to cause the overthrow of the existing Nicaraguan government.

Q. Thank you, Mr. MacMichael.

MS. BAIRD: I have no more questions.

THE COURT: Mr. Bradley?

MR. BRADLEY: No questions, Your Honor.

THE COURT: Very well. Thank you very much, Mr. MacMichael.

RICHARD GARFIELD, being duly sworn by the Court Officer to tell the truth, the whole truth and nothing but the truth, testified as follows:

Direct Examination by MS. BAIRD:

Q. Would you state your name?

A. Richard Marvin Garfield.

Q. Where do you live?

A. In New York City.

Q. What is your occupation?

A. I'm an infectious disease epidemiologist, a public health researcher.

Q. And are you also a nurse?

A. Yes.

Q. Where did you receive your education?

A. My nurse's education I received in Philadelphia. My Master's in Public Health I'm finishing this month from Columbia University, where I also work.

Q. Are you working on your Doctoral thesis now?

A. Yes.

Q. What is that on?

A. The thesis has to do with community participation in malaria-control activities in Nicaragua.

Q. Did your education and research lead you to Central America?

A. Yes.

Q. When was that?

A. In 1980, I visited Nicaragua and did a consultancy for the Ministry of Health in health practice and the organization of their health care system.

Q. What was the government of Nicaragua in 1980?

A. It was what is commonly called the Sandinista government.

Q. The present government of Nicaragua?

A. Well, the present government is an elected government. That was a government which had the same personnel but was not elected.

Q. That was the government that had taken power after Somoza?

A. Yes.

Q. Did your family also have ties to Somoza?

A. Well, ties is not exactly the term. My mother is a business woman. She's done business throughout Latin America for twenty years, and was a friend of Somoza.

Q. Your interest in Nicaragua goes back for some years, is that correct?

A. Yes. My going to Nicaragua was both professional, in that I was interested in working in public health, and personal, in that I had ties through my mother to business people and friends of hers.

Q. Did you have any strong political opinions about Nicaragua before you went there?

A. My opinion about Nicaragua before I went there was that it was an interesting place which was badly in need of help and had the possibility of economic and health development. I wanted to explore that possibility.

Q. Were there programs that the Nicaraguan government was undertaking that were of interest to you?

A. It was the general approach that they were beginning in 1980 which was unique. They were starting at that time to build a public health system, the likes of which had never existed there before.

Q. What do you mean by public health system?

A. Well, prior to 1979 there had been a severe shortage of doctors, hospital beds, and primary care centers except for the twelve percent of the population which had either private insurance or Social Security coverage. Beginning in 1979, and expanding in 1980 when I was first there, they were rapidly developing a health system which would reach much more of the population. Within the first four years of the new government the number of visits per population to a physician more than doubled and the number of immunizations quadrupled.

Q. By immunizations you mean against . . .

A. Polio, diphtheria, tetanus, measles. The number of primary health care centers tripled in a four-year period. It went from 157 to more than four hundred fifty. These are a few of the indicators of a profoundly rapid expansion in the services available to the population.

Q. What about the infant mortality rate?

A. We measured in Nicaragua in the first five years of the new government a reduction of thirty-seven percent in the infant mortality rate. The infant mortality rate in the public health field is considered the most sensitive. It is notable that no faster rate of decline in infant mortality has been reported in any other country, ever. I said reported; it's possible it has existed, but we don't have data from any country that shows a faster decline. This is a result of the expansion of the formal health system, the doctors and the clinics, and the expansion of the availability of prescriptions to a population which had never had access to that kind of thing before. Especially, it is a result of community participation in many different kinds of health activities, the immunizations and sanitation campaigns and other health education activities.

Q. How long were you in Nicaragua?

A. In 1980, I visited twice; the first time for four weeks and the second time for two weeks. In 1981, I lived there on a resident visa for nine months. In 1983, I spent six months working there. And my last visit to Nicaragua was during June and July, 1984.

Q. Did your trip to Nicaragua foster an interest in their anti-malaria campaign?

A. Well, as an employee of the Ministry of Health I was involved in many different activities, but late in 1981 the largest of a series of health campaigns occurred and many of us got involved in it. In fact, ten percent of the population of the country, most of them volunteers but also health professionals, got involved in a massive campaign against malaria. I got involved and that's when my particular interest in malaria began.

Q. What kind of things did this program do?

A. That specific campaign was an attempt to medicate the general population of the country for a three-day period in order to achieve a prophylaxis of malaria. The goal was to get a high level of coverage in the population so that the chance of disease transmission would be shut off for a short period of time, thereby reducing the disease. In 1981, they had an epidemic of malaria going on throughout Central America, particularly Nicaragua, because of the breakdown of the society and the health system, and the revolutionary war in 1978 and 1979. So this was an attempt to get everybody involved in a three-day campaign to rapidly reduce the number of cases.

Q. Was there opposition to this campaign?

A. There was. The campaign was unique. No such campaign had been tried on that scale in the world before. The rightist newspaper, *La Prensa*, which is a private opposition newspaper . . .

Q. Which operates freely or underground, or what?

A. It operates openly under the censorship law. All the papers are legal and kids sell them on the street all the time. That newspaper had an article several weeks before the three days in which the population was being encouraged to take the anti-malaria drugs and listed side effects of the drugs. It said that it's known that women faint and die away; that children may become crazy. They were reporting that these were scientifically documented side effects, and it's not true.

Q. Was there other opposition as well?

A. Yes, the clandestine contra radio operating out of Honduras broadcast these same charges and also broadcast that the malaria pills were from Russia and were for brainwashing. They actually said on the radio that the pills could make you into a Communist.

Q. Notwithstanding the opposition, was the malaria campaign successful or unsuccessful, in your opinion?

A. It was highly successful; seventy percent of the population took the anti-malaria drugs for the three-day period. In a population of about three million people, that's six million doses of drugs, by far the largest mass drug administration campaign for any disease ever to be carried out in the world. It was successful in an organizational sense. It was also successful in rapidly reducing the number of malaria cases for a four-month period.

Q. During your travels in Nicaragua did you visit the war zones there?

A. Yes. In 1981 we didn't identify them as war zones; they were areas where there was some occasional fighting, but the scale of hostilities was not such that we would have identified it in that way.

Q. Since that time have they come to be defined as war zones?

A. Well, yes. In 1983, when I was working there the contra military activity stepped up greatly and became permanent so that it became identified in Nicaragua as an ongoing war rather than occasional attacks.

Q. Where are these zones?

A. In December of 1983, the Minister of Defense of Nicaragua formally identified the war zones. The country is divided into sixteen different states. He identified, and I concur from my own personal observation of what's going on, that the states of Jinotega, Madriz, Nueva Segovia and Chinandega in the north bordering Honduras, the states of Rivas and Rio San Juan in the south bordering Costa Rica, and the state of Zelaya which is in the Atlantic coastal region, were military areas. I think that comes up to eight.

Q. Did you visit these zones?

A. Not all of them. I visited Jinotega, Chinandega, Zelaya and Rivas.

Q. Was there evidence of combat there?

A. Yes. In 1981 I did not personally see evidence of combat, although I learned of the deaths of some of the other employees of the Ministry of Health in those areas.

Q. Were they your friends?

A. The individuals who died in 1981 were not. I had known of them. I had seen them in meetings but I didn't have personal acquaintance with any of them. In 1983 when I returned and worked in Nicaragua I visited some of those northern states several times and evidence of the war was obvious.

Q. What kind of evidence?

A. The evidence that I saw included the destruction of grain storage sites and municipal offices in villages and in the town of Ocotal. A contra attack on the day of George Shultz's visit to Nicaragua in 1984 involved strafing the hospital in the City of Ocotal.

Q. Are there many hospitals in Nicaragua?

A. There are a total of forty-three hospitals in Nicaragua. Most of them are small affairs, though. There are seven major hospitals. In the regions up along the border the hospitals are regional referral centers of medium size. The Ocotal Hospital, for instance, has an operating room and several of the bullets from the attack are lodged in that operating room.

Q. What other evidence did you see of combat in those areas?

A. Houses that were destroyed.

Q. Did you form an opinion as to the targets of the contras?

A. I did.

Q. What is that?

A. Through observation and discussions with people it became obvious that there were different targets. One was the peasantry. It is reported that through June of 1984, 853 civilians have been killed by the contras in Nicaragua. Slightly more than half of them were peasants.

Q. By peasants you mean poor farmers?

A. Individual farmers without large plots. Also included in the peasant population are farmers on cooperatives which are privately-owned collectives. They are, for the most part, poor.

Q. You mentioned that there were other targets of the contras.

A. Another target clearly was government employees.

Q. Like yourself?

A. Well, I never personally felt myself to be a target, but . . .

Q. Were you ever under attack?

A. By happenstance, yes. The attack was not on me, but my home in Managua is near the international airport and a contra plane from Honduras bombed it with five hundred pound bombs in August of 1983, in the early morning hours. There was a giant explosion which broke windows. We didn't quite get knocked out of bed, but with the boom and all, we got knocked all around.

Q. Your house remained standing?

A. Yes.

Q. Going back to the war zones, you mentioned the second target was government officials; what do you mean by government officials?

A. Well, to finish answering your prior question, I personally wasn't a target but two of the physicians that were killed were our people, one was French and one was German. The targets were apparently not limited to Nicaraguans, but included those who represented the Nicaraguan government in some form. In a broader answer to the question, twenty-two employees of the Ministry of Health — nurses, doctors and technicians — plus some fifty health volunteers in the villages have been killed. There are a reported 158 deaths, at the hands of the contras, among adult education teachers and students, agricultural extension workers, and personnel of the telephone company who were laying lines into the rural villages. Almost all attacks are in rural, isolated areas.

Q. Did you see any effect on the malaria campaign from these attacks?

A. Yes, the effect is quite clear. There's been a sixty-six percent reduction in the number of malaria cases in the eight states which are not under attack. Normally every year during the rainy season the number of malaria cases curves up. The transmission of the disease has gone down so much it's like a flat line, you no longer get this curve. This is unique among countries which have a chronic malaria problem. We see in the areas where there's peace that these health activities are profoundly successful, more successful than any of us would have hoped. In the war zone areas, however, with the disruptions caused by the contras, the killing of anti-malaria workers, cutting of roads, terrorization of volunteers in the local villages, it has been impossible to implement, extensively or consistently, these local malaria measures. And we note from August of 1983 until the present time, an epidemic of malaria in the war zone. This became very noticeable to us because it was in June of 1983 when the contra attacks really stepped up and became a permanent war. For these and other more technical reasons, we can count twenty-five hundred excess cases that are a result of the war. We consider that a minimum number, however, since in fact malaria is slowly disappearing in the rest of the country.

Q. I know your main interest in Nicaragua is in malaria, but did you notice other medical problems in the areas that are now under attack?

A. Fifty-four clinics and health posts and one hospital have been either destroyed completely, destroyed partially, or abandoned because of an inability to provide protection to the health workers. This is the primary health care system, available to those who have an illness and want to go get care. Particularly, this is the system for the rural and the poor, since they can't get to the hospitals in the cities. The average person, who was beginning to get health benefits for the first time, no longer has access to modern medical care. In addition, because of the injuries caused by the war, many of the routine kinds of care that were available in the regional hospitals, like the hospital in Ocotal, have been cut back. When I visited that hospital in the summer of 1984, a quarter of the beds held individuals who had war-related injuries. Because of the fear of large-scale attacks they have decided to keep as many beds empty as possible, and so, anybody who has an illness that they think is going to last longer than five days cannot be kept at those hospitals. They have to find their way to the capital city because they want to reserve the bed for war-related injuries. This means that even where health facilities are open there is a cutback in the accessibility of services, curative and preventive.

Q. How about psychological results?

A. It is reported that there have been a total of 2,609 individuals killed so far in the war in Nicaragua. There were 1,755 military deaths and 853 civilian deaths, a very high number for such a small country. I was in a neighborhood in Nicaragua which has one of the six mental health clinics which have been set up in the last two years. The medical director of this clinic said to me that most of the patients she sees now are individuals with severe depression, and that three-quarters of the individuals who were seen in recent months had lost a family member recently due to the war. That's the most concrete expression I can give to the kind of psychological results of the war on those who have not been killed.

Q. When you came back from Nicaragua did you have different political opinions than when you left?

A. Well, I won't say that they have changed in any fundamental sense. I went overseas to work knowing that health development is difficult and long-term, and that there are many conflicts along the way. No one who goes to Nicaragua could imagine that everything was going to be smooth sailing. I knew that it was possible that the United States would get more heavily involved in activities against Nicaragua because at the time that I went the contras were already being trained by the United States. However, to see the massive destruction on a daily basis, and to see the whole story turned around in the United States, so that what is actually going on, in my observation, is virtually unavailable to the public in the United States, I think that has affected my views. I won't say changed, but they have matured considerably. I couldn't imagine that you could pull the wool over the people's eyes this much and get away with it. And I couldn't imagine that the U.S. would get involved in such dirty tricks. A few dirty tricks, yes, but like this, I couldn't imagine it.

Q. Have you become politically active since you returned to the United States?

A. Yes. I am a member of the New York State Nurses Association Human Rights Council. Our State Nurses Association and the National Nurses Association are quite concerned about the contra attacks against neutral activities, such as providing health care to civilians, which are covered by the Geneva Accords. We are looking for ways to assure that civilians are not made targets in the war. Also, I might note that my other professional organization, the American Public Health Association, a year ago passed a resolution at its convention applauding the considerable and unique advances in health and welfare of the population of Nicaragua — an unusual kind of an act for an association which deals with seatbelts and clean water. But the improvements in health were so dramatic and provided a model for poor countries that was so remarkable that the association went on record as supporting it. I have been involved in providing information and assisting people to find legislative and social ways to educate the American public. Many people in the organization, including myself, feel that if the public knew what is going on, it would not permit it.

Q. And if our congresspeople knew what is going on?

A. I don't think any North American who really knew what was going on, perhaps even Ronald Reagan, would go along with it.

MS. BAIRD: Thank you very much.

THE COURT: Thank you, Ms. Baird. Mr. Bradley?

Cross-Examination by MR. BRADLEY:

Q. Mr. Garfield, since your trips to Central America have you contacted any congressmen?

A. Yes.

Q. Can you tell the jury who they are please?

A. Well, I have met twice with the staff of Senator Moynihan of New York. I have written to Senator Ted Weiss, my senator in New York as well.

Q. Have you received responses from them?

A. Yes.

Q. What are their feelings with respect to the American involvement in Central America?

A. Senator Weiss is a strong proponent of my position, which is that we should not be aiding contras if they're going to be involved in terrorist activities. He's become one of the strongest proponents of that position in Congress, and the response of his office was very favorable and appreciative. The office of Senator Moynihan appears to be interested in getting more full information. The Senator, in my opinion, has waffled on issues related to Central America. His staff has said that they agree that civilians should not be under attack, yet he hasn't always voted that way. I think that he is inconsistent. That's the reason we went back and talked to them again.

Q. Is it fair to say that, in your opinion, in Congress there is a great difference of opinion as to American involvement in Central America?

A. There are certainly differences of opinion, but I see a general trend. I think it's impossible not to see a trend; clearly the White House is pushing for quite a bit of aid to the contras and the votes in Congress have not been very favorable to the White House.

Q. Has the administration been successful in getting some aid to go to Central America?

A. Well, they have sent a hundred million dollars worth of aid.

Q. Thank you.

MR. BRADLEY: No further questions, Your Honor.

THE COURT: Thank you. Ms. Baird, anything further?

MS. BAIRD: Nothing.

THE COURT: Very well. Thank you very much, sir.

ERIC BROQUE, having been duly sworn to tell the truth, the whole truth and nothing but the truth, testified as follows:

Direct Examination by MS. BAIRD:

Q. State your name, please.

A. My name is Eric Broque.

Q. And your address?

A. I live in Burlington, Vermont.

Q. Eric, you're one of the Defendants here; is that right?

A. That's correct.

Q. Eric, what is your current employment?

A. At the moment I work at the University of Vermont as Business Manager and prior to that I was employed by the State of Vermont in the Department of Corrections.

Q. When did you first start getting interested in Central America?

A. It was almost a year ago today when I heard a minister who is living in exile in the Boston area speak about the situation in Nicaragua. That was the first time I had been informed about the severity of the situation and he expressed very clearly and very convincingly that the Nicaraguan people were expecting a U.S. invasion of their country by Christmas of 1983. At that time I learned about a program called Witness for Peace, that you have heard a little bit about already, which was sending delegations from every state in the United States, common everyday people to prevent some of the atrocities in that country.

Q. And did you follow up on this interest?

A. Yes. After much reflection on and learning about the plans and the program of Witness for Peace, I traveled to Nicaragua in early February of 1984, as a member of the Vermont/New Hampshire delegation.

Q. Who was in that delegation with you?

A. The delegation consisted of seventeen Vermonters, individuals from New Hampshire, and a woman from Philadelphia. Among them were five ministers of various denominations. Witness for Peace is a spiritually-based group that has a great concern about the acts that are being perpetrated against the government of Nicaragua by the contras.

Q. Were your motives at all religiously-based?

A. I would say that there is a very strong spiritual commitment to peace and to justice for many of the people in that group.

Q. And that's true of you personally?

A. Very much so. I think that my participation on the trip and in the actions in March were for me very much an act of conscience and part of my obligation to act on behalf of my brothers and sisters in the world.

Q. I take it when you were down there you spoke with some Nicaraguans. Did they make any requests of you?

A. Well, we had three purposes in making our trip. The first, as you have heard, was to maintain a presence of North Americans in the zone of conflict. The witness is continuing to discourage the contras from attacking. Another purpose of the trip was to be a witness in the event an attack did occur. And the third important part was to return to this country and share our experiences with people. We have done that since we have been back, both in the community as well as with Congressional representatives.

Q. On that last purpose of your visit, did you speak with Nicaraguans about that?

A. Once we had been in the country for a period of time and heard people's stories and had spoken with many, many people in the countryside and in the city, we were very concerned. We were all very moved by their experiences and what their lives were like. And we had great concern among us as to what would be the most effective way to act on what we had learned. What could we do to bring an end to the continued U.S. military support for the contras? We asked people continuously, because many of us were feeling at the time that perhaps we should not return to the U.S. We had a very strong sense of commitment and we felt perhaps we shouldn't return to our lives in this country. Perhaps it would be better to stay in Nicaragua and to keep doing that kind of work. We asked people in the countryside, what would you have us do to bring peace to your country? We asked the same question of the Minister of Interior, whom we had the pleasure of meeting. They felt the important work needed to be done in the United States. They appreciated our coming, and it was important for us to educate ourselves and to see the reality of Nicaragua, but the most important work that we could do was to return to the United States and speak with our friends and neighbors and particularly to address our congresspeople. We could provide better information than they had been receiving through normal channels, and also plead with them to put an end to the war.

Q. When did you get back to the United States?

A. We arrived back in mid-February, 1984.

Q. I take it as one of the Defendants, you freely admit that you were present in Senator Stafford's office; is that correct?

A. That's right. I was there on Monday morning.

Q. Can you tell us about your intentions through the weekend, from Friday through Monday?

A. I had learned about the plan to make a plea to the Senator to reconsider his position. After much reflection I had decided that I had an obligation of conscience to continue the work I had begun, and to be present for that activity on Friday afternoon. Unfortunately, on Wednesday of that week something came up and I was unable to be present on Friday.

Q. What was it that came up?

A. My mother, who lives alone in New York, had been mugged and I went to take care of her for that weekend and to make arrangements for her further care.

Q. And when did you get back to Burlington?

A. I got back to Burlington on Monday morning to return to work, and on learning that many people were still at Senator Stafford's office and that there had not been a response to our request from him, I went to his office. I arrived there around ten-thirty in the morning.

Q. So the only time you were there was Monday, and the earliest time was ten-thirty in the morning?

A. That's correct.

Q. And you were arrested when?

A. I believe it was between eleven and noon on that day.

Q. So you were there from ten-thirty to noon?

A. At most. It was at most an hour and a half.

Q. Business hours?

A. Exactly.

Q. You have heard the remarks of Ray Pecor and Rey Post, and Officer Lawrence, asking you to leave?

A. That's correct.

Q. And you stayed?

A. Yes, I stayed.

Q. Would it be fair to say that you stayed in part because of what the people of Nicaragua asked you to do?

A. Absolutely. It was very present in our minds that morning. I had recently come back from Nicaragua. To this day the memory is still very clear in my mind, that suffering is a part of the daily life of the people in the zones of conflict in Nicaragua and El Salvador. In their daily lives they carry great burdens. In a relative sense the consequences of our acts were fairly minimal and we felt a strong obligation to continue expressing our solidarity with our brothers and sisters in Central America.

Q. Do you feel that you had lawful authority to be where you were even after you were told to leave?

A. Absolutely; both in a legal sense that it's my senator's office and I was there during office hours and I was petitioning on a critical issue, but also on moral grounds, considering that there were unspeakable acts of terrorism which required ending.

MS. BAIRD: No further questions.

THE COURT: Mr. Bradley?

MR. BRADLEY: Thank you, Your Honor.

Cross-Examination by MR. BRADLEY:

Q. Mr. Broque, to your knowledge, prior to March 26th, had Senator Stafford had any open meetings with any of the people in Vermont about Central America?

A. I believe, unlike the other two Congressional representatives, he had not held an open meeting.

Q. So when you were informed on Monday morning that he was willing to meet with a small delegation of you, you didn't perceive that as being an opportunity that you should take advantage of?

A. That's correct. We thought that it was important for all Vermonters to have access to the Senator on an equal basis, and we wanted to insure that he would hear many voices and not just a few.

Q. So you were not willing to accept this first offer by Senator Stafford, as a concession on his part and an opening to future open public forums?

A. In fact, the offer was a refusal. It was a refusal to have an open meeting, and in place of that he offered us the closed meeting.

Q. So it was all or nothing at that point?

A. We were there for the open meeting, having withdrawn several other requests of the Senator.

Q. So you didn't get what you wanted, so you were going to refuse to leave?

A. We refused to leave unless there was an agreement that at some point in the future, at the Senator's convenience, he would meet with his constituents in an open way.

Q. Unless Senator Stafford agreed to do exactly what you wanted him to do you were not going to leave his office?

A. I don't believe it was that exactly. I think there was a great deal of flexibility.

Q. Where was that flexibility?

A. In terms of scheduling and how the forum might be held, and how it might be arranged.

Q. And his willingness to meet with a smaller number was not in your flexibility?

A. Meeting with a small number of us wasn't the issue. It was having an open forum.

MR. BRADLEY: No other questions, Your Honor.

THE COURT: Mr. Nelson, anything further?

MR. NELSON: Nothing further, Your Honor.

THE COURT: Very good. Thank you very much, sir.

Next witness?

JOHN McCULLOUGH: We call John Stockwell.

JOHN STOCKWELL, having been duly sworn to tell the truth, the whole truth and nothing but the truth, testified as follows:

Direct Examination by MR. McCULLOUGH:

Q. Would you state your name and address, please?

A. John Stockwell. I live in Austin, Texas.

Q. And what is your educational background?

A. A Liberal Arts degree from the University of Texas.

Q. Where did you go after that?

A. I did three years in the Marine Corps, Marine Officers Basic School. I served in the Second Force Reconnaissance Company, and then I did a total of nineteen years with the Marine Corps including reserve time.

Q. What was the nature of your duties with the Marine Corps?

A. I was an Intelligence Reconnaissance Officer with a paramilitary specialty. I did cruises in the Caribbean and a cruise off the coast of Africa. This was in the early '60s.

Q. When you say you were reconnaissance specialist, what does that mean?

A. Strategic reconnaissance means putting teams in a country from a distance, such as parachuting in or from submarines. It was primarily long-range patrols to gather intelligence.

Q. Does this mean you were basically a spy while you were in the Marines?

A. I was an intelligence officer. There is, by the way, a technical difference.

Q. Oh, is there?

A. Yes. A spy would be someone you recruit, who might be a part of another government, and an intelligence officer, in a military sense, is doing military missions. You can't shoot a military intelligence officer if he's doing his job in uniform. You can't shoot him or try him as being a spy.

Q. I'm sure that was a great comfort to you. Did there come a time when you became employed by the CIA?

A. In 1964 I was working for the Marine Corps in Denver, Colorado, and the CIA approached me by letter. They were interested in my background. My father had been an engineer contracted by the Presbyterian Church to build hydroelectric plants in the Belgian Congo and I had spent some years there, and so I knew something of Africa and spoke some languages. And that, combined with my military background, interested the CIA very much. The Congo was in high rebellion in 1964. The CIA had a large mercenary army fighting under Colonel Mobutu, and they were very much interested in my background and expertise.

Q. What did you do while you were in the CIA?

A. I went through a year's training as a case officer. I then went overseas. I did six years in Africa, three countries, three tours. I rose to Chief of Base, and then Chief of Station which is equivalent more or less to ambassador. Then I had a tour at headquarters in the United States. Then I was in Vietnam up-country from 1973 to '75. I came out with the evacuation in April of '75. My last substantial job with the agency before I resigned, was in 1975 and '76. I was the Chief of the Paramilitary Task Force. It's the Commander, if you will, of the forces of the CIA that ran the covert action in Angola. It was bigger than the Nicaraguan covert action and quite similar to it. It didn't last as long but at the outset it was larger.

Q. When you say the Nicaraguan covert action, you mean what is going on now?

A. What the CIA has been doing in Nicaragua since 1980, under President Carter.

Q. I gather the position you held for a number of years in the CIA is considered a pretty high position?

A. At the end I was a GS-14. That's about the equivalent of Colonel. I sat on a Subcommittee of the National Security Council to manage this operation in Angola. My job was in Washington. However, I had forces working in Angola and other parts of the world.

Q. And who were you directly reporting to?

A. I was reporting directly to Jim Potts, the African Division Chief of the GASA team, and I worked directly with CIA Division Chiefs. These were the individuals who were managing the program under the National Security Council and Henry Kissinger.

Q. Was part of your job in the CIA producing information reports either for your superiors or for other people in and outside of the government?

A. Absolutely. The intelligence officer part of what I did, as opposed to paramilitary, was to gather information and to process it and prepare it for the policy makers, including of course, my own supervisors.

Q. So who would be the audience for that kind of information?

A. Essentially you're developing information for the use of the policy makers in the United States government; the White House, the State Department and many other branches of the government that have an interest in the country that you're covering. You do, however, have another function. Other types of reports we developed were directed at the American public.

Q. So as to inform the American public of the actions of the CIA, and the various forces in the . . .

A. Not exactly to inform, but rather to create an impression in their minds of the country that you're targeting.

Q. I see. Were these reports produced by you at the request of your supervisors or was it just part of your daily job?

A. Well, it's both. It's part of your daily job but when you're working in a dramatic operation like the Angolan operation, you're working very closely with your supervisors in the National Security Council, but especially with your supervisors in the CIA. You're having meetings continuously. You're talking to them about the approach, the deployment, the lines, the cover stories, the reports that you will publish.

Q. And I take it you probably had a staff working for you?

A. When the thing was over, I wrote commendations for about one hundred forty people that worked for me.

Q. Is that the total number of people that worked for you, or is that a smaller number who were deserving of commendations?

A. That was just about the total of CIA staffers. Now, that did not include the Africans and Europeans. We had literally thousands of people in the program, including the soldiers we recruited, and the mercenaries.

Q. I assume you weren't generating this information yourself; that was done by your staff?

A. It was a staff effort. I was supervising it.

Q. And what portion of your staff was actually involved in production of this information?

A. Well, one-third of my staff. We had three units. We had one that was paramilitary that delivered trainers, arms, and mercenaries into Angola. We had one that was intelligence, what they call foreign intelligence case officers, who were gathering information and delivering it to the policy makers. And one-third of the staff was professional propagandists whose job was to write articles and create movies and insert them into the media, the western and United States media, to create the impression in people's minds that we wanted them to know about what was going on in Angola.

Q. So for example, they write an article and get it published in American newspapers?

MR. BRADLEY: Objection, Your Honor. I'm not sure what relevance this particular line of questioning has. The point of interest for us is Central America.

THE COURT: Mr. McCullough, what is the relevancy?

MR. McCULLOUGH: Your Honor, we will be indicating by Mr. Stockwell's testimony, that the type of activity he is describing is part of an overall plan and habit of the CIA of generating information which is then fed to the American public and government.

THE COURT: How will it be tied into the situation you're addressing?

MR. McCULLOUGH: By Mr. Stockwell's testimony that he's familiar with it.

THE COURT: Very well. We will take it subject to being struck if it's not tied in.

Direct Examination continued by MR. McCULLOUGH:

Q. The question was, did one of these activities involve getting articles into American newspapers?

A. Yes. The job of one-third of my staff, the professional writers and professional film people, was to introduce stories into the media. They worked at it continuously, and they were continuously successful in creating the illusion that the Soviets and the Cubans were moving to take over Angola and in creating the illusion that the United States' position was defensible and that we were trying to stay out. This was exactly the opposite of the truth. The United States went into Angola first and at each new step of escalation in the fighting the Soviets and Cubans were responding to our initiative. We got stories into newspapers around the western world and across this country. Stories, for example, of Cuban soldiers raping African women. We had them captured in a battle and executed by firing squads of African women. And there had been no rapes. It was totally fictitious, and yet we managed to get this story picked up by most newspapers in this country and abroad.

Q. Did your job also involve preparing reports for the legislative and the executive branch of government?

A. Yes, indeed. The CIA Director was required by the House to brief the Congressional committees. He gave formal briefings to each committee and some less formal briefings. I was working with him, advising him of what we were doing, and he and the other managers of the program were deciding how they would handle the Congress. I was present in the meetings in which they worked out the party line, if you will, which was . . .

Q. Without getting into the specifics at this point, what general types of information were included in these briefings?

A. Well, the CIA Director deceived Congress on some very important questions they were asking. Questions like: were we involved with the South African army that was fighting in Angola? It would have been a felony for us to be so involved because there was a law against it. We were deeply involved with them, coordinating all kinds of military details, and the Director assured Congress that we were not, that we were staying well away from them. We were involved with the white mercenaries that were being hired to kill blacks inside the black African country of Angola. He said we had nothing to do with them. In fact, we had sent people overseas to recruit and deliver into Angola four units of mercenaries to fight and kill there. There were other categories equally specific in which the CIA Director lied to Congress.

Q. These briefings made by the CIA Director were composed of information that you provided to the Director?

A. We briefed the Director. We were working under his supervision. We were not in a position of deceiving him. He knew what we were doing. He was ordering us to do it. And then we would work with him to decide what to tell the Congress.

Q. So you had actual discussions with the Director or close aides?

A. Yes.

Q. Were you able to learn the reason that the CIA made this kind of misstatement to the government?

A. I certainly was involved enough in situations to understand why the Director and the Department of Defense and the African Division Chief gave false briefings. The rationale was simply that we would not have been permitted to do what we were doing if the truth had been known. If either the Congress or the American people had known what we were doing we would have been stopped. It was something that the CIA, the National Security Council, and Henry Kissinger very much wanted to do; and so the lies were tailored to create an atmosphere where the Congress would not stop us, but instead would encourage us and give us money.

Q. In the course of your employment at the CIA, did you come to learn whether the CIA had a general practice of providing false information to Congress?

A. Absolutely. The CIA had a position of antagonism with Congressional oversight. We did not feel, the managers of the CIA did not feel, that the Congress had a right to penetrate CIA secrets and techniques, and to know what it was doing. We felt like the CIA had a responsibility to itself to deceive the Congress. You have to remember, for example, that CIA Director, Dick Helms, was indicted for lying to Congress about the Shilly Operation and was actually punished for it.

Q. Are you familiar with CIA involvement in other countries? In particular, I'd now like to focus on Nicaragua.

A. Yes, I believe so. I was in Vietnam. I had years in Africa. Since I left the government I have traveled to Nicaragua seven times to educate myself; to see a major covert action. It was an opportunity to go inside a country that we were attacking through a covert action, to talk to the leaders and the victims, the people who are injured, the women who are raped. It's a different view, I might say, than you get from the seventeenth floor of Langley Headquarters in Washington.

Q. Did you have contact while you were in the CIA with the Nicaragua desk managers?

A. Yes. There were many of us on the same floor. I knew the Nicaragua desk managers. We would have lunch together.

Q. Would you describe what a desk is?

A. A desk would mean an officer, or two, or twenty-five, depending on the country. The Nicaragua desk was not too large. I went down there on occasion and sat with them and they talked to me about the nature of their operations. I left the CIA before the Sandinista revolution took over in Nicaragua, so they were describing to me the nature of the CIA's relations with the Somoza government.

Q. And what was the nature of CIA relations?

A. A close liaison, primarily with Somoza's Police and his Guard. I was actually considering getting myself assigned to be Chief of Station in Nicaragua so I was quite interested in what was going on there. The desk described it to me. They said they didn't have too much going there because it was a —

MR. BRADLEY: Objection, Your Honor; this is hearsay.

THE COURT: Mr. McCullough?

MR. McCULLOUGH: Your Honor, I think I have established that Mr.

Stockwell has developed sufficient expertise in the operations of the CIA to testify about these activities of the CIA.

THE COURT: Objection overruled. Go ahead, sir.

A I informed myself of the nature of the CIA's relations with the Somoza government. I would prefer not to go into specifics, names and details, but in general it consisted of a close liaison with the police and with the National Guard.

Q. Was that desk also involved in providing the kind of reports about Nicaragua that you were providing for Angola?

A. Definitely, although we had a covert action going in Angola and at that time there was no covert action going in Nicaragua. It was a liaison with an existing government, so the flow of intelligence reports about Nicaragua to the U.S. government was routine. And the production of propaganda would be more routine instead of a special focus on a special country.

Q. But it did still involve the production of false information?

A. Absolutely. This is a major function of the CIA. They focus on countries that are under attack or needing support. The CIA has one floor of an entire wing that has the function of producing propaganda and putting it into the U.S. media to influence the American people's minds about the situation in a country. This information is not accurate. If it were accurate it could be produced by scholars or published by the government.

Q. Now, are you able to assess from your years of involvement with the CIA, the extent of CIA influence in, or control over, United States foreign policy?

A. My analysis of this is that it runs about sixty percent in normal circumstances and it's totally dominant in specific situations.

Q. What type of situation would that be?

A. In Angola, for example, Ambassador Nathaniel Davis, who should have been the individual who formulated U.S. policy towards Angola, had an opposite policy from our covert action. He said we should stay out. We should work with the effective leadership of Angola, which is the MPLA forces that we fought against. The CIA created enough pressure that he had to resign his position because he disagreed with our policy and he got himself named for a retirement job as Ambassador to Switzerland. There was another embassy staffer who was the only U.S. official who had personal contact with all of the Angola leaders. He vigorously supported Ambassador Davis and said that we should work with the MPLA as being the best-educated and best-qualified to run the country. He was behind the lines of the fighting, so the CIA sent a cable to him that was patently false, lying to him about the U.S. position so he wouldn't know the truth about the war we were waging, so he wouldn't be in a position to protest or make public statements or contradict us or embarrass us.

In regard to Nicaragua, the assessment of the Congressional Oversight Committee as reported in the *New York Times* is that the CIA is totally dominant. If the Secretary of State, according to the *New York Times*, does not kowtow to the CIA line, he isn't invited to the meetings to hammer out policy decisions.

Q. So are you saying the CIA is actually conducting its own foreign policy?

A. I'm saying that it's dominant. It dominates the invisible government. It dominates foreign policy by a factor of about sixty percent and completely in situations like Central America.

Q. In total disregard of the State Department or Congress?

A. They steamroll them. And the members of the State Department or Congress who don't cooperate are just shut out of the process.

Q. You briefly mentioned earlier the use of mercenaries in Angola. We have heard some other testimony about mercenaries. Were you actually involved in handling mercenaries?

A. At different times in my career I dealt with CIA mercenaries.

Q. Who are mercenaries?

A. Mercenaries, as defined by the CIA, are foreigners who work for you for money.

Q. How do you go out and find mercenaries?

A. Well, for one of the programs we had in Angola we worked through Colonel Kasto, a Portuguese Colonel, who had fought in Angola and knew a lot of Portuguese soldiers. We hired him and paid him a total of three hundred thousand dollars to recruit a force of Portuguese veterans and deliver them into Angola for us.

Q. So they were the remnant of the previous power structure?

A. Yes. Another one was Bob Denard, the French adventurer, who recruited French veterans for us to go in and fight. Most of them had previous colonial experience as well.

Q. Is it against the law for you to hire mercenaries, do you know?

A. The United States law prohibits recruiting Americans.

MR. BRADLEY: Objection, Your Honor. I don't know if this witness can testify as to what the law is.

THE COURT: Mr. McCullough?

MR. McCULLOUGH: How about if I ask him if he knows what the law is?

THE COURT: No, the law in this courtroom is for me. Objection is sustained.

Direct Examination continued by MR. McCULLOUGH:

Q. Let me ask you one more question then, Mr. Stockwell. You have described the CIA as controlling foreign policy in a number of areas around the world, and providing false information about what it's doing to the legislative branch of government as well as the American people. Now, if this is all going on how would it be possible for any U.S. citizen to exercise influence or control over the foreign policy of their government?

A. Well, it's definitely possible, but the citizens have to force the thing out into the open. They have to take action — lobbying, demonstrations — so that the public knowledge and awareness of what's happening begins to override the propaganda, and people begin to see through and reject the propaganda. This has happened before. It happened during the Vietnam war specifically. It happened during the Angolan operations specifically.

Q. Thank you.

MR. McCULLOUGH: No further questions.

THE COURT: Thank you, Mr. McCullough. Mr. Bradley?

Cross-Examination by MR. BRADLEY:

Q. Mr. Stockwell, when did you say you stopped working for the Central Intelligence Agency?

A. In 1977.

Q. And you did state that you have been in Central America seven times?

A. Yes.

Q. Was that in an official capacity?

A. No, that's as a writer, as an authority, as a lecturer on the subject.

Q. Why did you leave the CIA?

A. I left the CIA because I decided that what it was doing was morally wrong and not in the United States' security interests.

Q. And how many years did you work for them?

A. Thirteen altogether.

Q. Thank you.

MR. BRADLEY: No further questions, Your Honor.

THE COURT: Thank you, Mr. Bradley. Mr. McCullough, anything further?

MR. McCULLOUGH: No, Your Honor.

THE COURT: Very well. Thank you very much, Mr. Stockwell. I appreciate your coming, sir. Court recessed for the day.

Open court, November 16th, 1984, eight-thirty a.m.

HOWARD ZINN, having been duly sworn to tell the truth, the whole truth and nothing but the truth, testified as follows:

Direct Examination by MR. McCULLOUGH:

Q. Mr. Zinn, would you tell the jury your name and address?

A. My name is Howard Zinn. I live in Auburndale, Massachusetts.

Q. And what do you do for a living?

A. I'm a Professor of Political Science at Boston University.

Q. Would you describe to the jury your educational background?

A. Well, I did my undergraduate work in History and English at New York University, I did my Master's degree work in History and Economics at Columbia University, and I did my Doctorate in History and Political Science, also at Columbia, and I did post-Doctoral work in East Asian studies at Harvard University.

Q. Is your major area of focus American history?

A. American history has been my major field.

Q. And do you have a specialization within the field of American history?

A. Well, I guess I have specialized in the history of social movements in the United States, the popular movements in American history.

Q. What do you mean by that, history's popular movements?

A. Well, I mean the history of movements which arose because of very deep-felt grievances, starting with the fight for independence from England, and also issues like slavery, the rights of working people, farmers, women, anti-war movements, blacks fighting against discrimination, movements like that.

Q. I know you weren't here earlier in the trial, but one of the witnesses, Philip Fiermonte, testified about national organizations, including the Central American Solidarity Association and the Coalition in Solidarity with the People of El Salvador, that have been working throughout the country to express their dissatisfaction with the national policy towards Central America. Are you at all familiar with what's been going on, on that front?

A. Yes.

Q. From your research into the history of social movements and your current knowledge of the movements which our Defendants are a part of, do you see any parallels with other movements in American history?

A. Well, social movements all through American history, including the current one dealing with problems in Central America, all use a variety of tactics. Their basic intention is to arouse public opinion. The idea is to try to get the public, which they usually believe has not been told the whole truth by the press or the government, aroused about an issue. They want to get information to the public. They want to appeal to the people who have not been paying attention to this issue. And so they use a variety of tactics which have been classic in American tradition, tactics of demonstration, tactics of petition, tactics of civil disobedience. By civil disobedience I mean the technical violation of law in order to try to bring to public attention some very powerful issue, some very fundamental principle. This is an approach which goes back to the American Revolutionary period, to the movements of that time when, as most everybody knows who has learned something about the American Revolution, the colonists in New England used a variety of tactics which were technically outside the law, but which the colonists believed fit in with what they called a higher law. When they went onto the property of stamp tax collectors and destroyed the stamps, when they violated property lines in various ways in order to bring the attention of people to the abuses of the British King and Parliament, they were appealing to fundamental principles of government which they then expressed in the Declaration of Independence.

The Declaration of Independence was really the summing up of what is the relationship between people and government. The basic idea of the Declaration was that government derived its power from people. People set up governments. People set them up for certain purposes, and the purposes were to do something for people to guarantee life, liberty and the pursuit of happiness. And that if such times arise in the history of a society where the government itself begins to act against the liberties of people, against the lives of people, then people have a right to assert these basic principles, to do things in defense of their rights, to disobey the government, to alter or abolish the government, as the Declaration of Independence put it. And therefore, by extension, to do those things which might not go so far as abolishing the government, but which would go so far as engaging in the technical violation of laws for these fundamental principles. That idea of social protest, of civil disobedience, was carried on into the movement against slavery.

The Fugitive Slave Act of 1793 said that any person who was enslaved, bound to labor in one state, who escaped into another state, should be returned to the state of enslavement. And there were a number of instances in which people who were opposed to slavery violated that Act. In 1830, in Boston, there was a case of a Baltimore man who came to Boston to find a slave who was living in Boston. The slave was brought into Federal Court and, presumably, they were going to enforce the Act. A group of people who were opposed to slavery rescued the person from the clutches of the slaveholder and they were never prosecuted.

The Fugitive Slave Act of 1850 was particularly outrageous because it not only provided for the slaves to be returned to their masters, but it almost ensured that they would not get a fair hearing to determine if they were slaves. In the year 1851 there were a number of instances where people violated the Fugitive Slave Act openly. They went to places where slaves were kept. They crossed boundary lines. They went into police stations. They went into buildings where slaves were being housed before being returned. They did it in a famous case in Pennsylvania in 1851. They did it in a case of a slave called Jerry in Syracuse in that same year. They did it in a case of a man named Shadrach in Boston. In all of those cases they rescued the slaves and then they were acquitted by juries, on the basis, I think, of the notion that they were doing something in keeping with the fundamental idea of the Declaration of Independence. That in violating a particular law they were adhering to the fundamental principles of American government and the American tradition; they were concerned about life and liberty and they were acting for that. In fact, a number of state governments cooperated with acts of civil disobedience. Vermont, Massachusetts, Maine, New Hampshire, Michigan, and several other states passed laws which said that their citizens or officials could not cooperate with the enforcement of the Fugitive Slave Act. I guess you would call it active civil disobedience by the state government against federal law. Vermont said they could not use Vermont public buildings to house slaves awaiting their hearings.

So this is the kind of thing that happened in that period. And it's fair to say that there was some kind of carry-over from that to the civil rights movement of our time. If you look at the life of Martin Luther King, he tells how as a freshman at Morehouse College in Atlanta, he read the essay on civil disobedience by Henry David Thoreau and he was astonished. It was the first time he had encountered the philosophical justification for those principles which he knew in his heart were right. That it was all right, on certain occasions, to disobey a law on behalf of some higher principle. The actions of the civil rights movement to do away with racial segregation in the 1950s and '60s were really based on the same idea. And when activists were brought into court you very often found the juries, judges, and sometimes prosecutors would recognize that their violation of law needed to be overlooked on behalf of some higher principle. In the 1960s there were a number of instances like this. In the case of *Gonner v. Louisiana* in 1961, Judge Harland made the point that a sit-in was a form of free speech. A few years later, in a case of trespassing in a restaurant, the point was made by the justices that the sit-in was, in some way, an acceptable form of free speech or free assembly. There was a case a few years after that, in 1966 in Louisiana, where Blacks sat in at a library which was segregated. Blacks could not go into the library. The Blacks went into the library and they sat down. They refused to move. They were arrested. The case came up before the Supreme Court and the Supreme Court said although they were violating the law, in this case the segregation law, there were times when it was necessary for people to make their point, as the Court put it, "by their silent and reproachful presence."

I'm sorry for taking you almost year-by-year through American history, but I just want to move very quickly through some of the major movements.

Most recently the movement against the war in Vietnam was a movement in which many technical violations of law were committed in an effort to affect public opinion. And when public opinion became aroused enough and awakened enough to the issue then the judges and juries began behaving in these cases in a way that seemed to recognize the principle of civil disobedience.

In a case in Camden, New Jersey, in 1973, the people had clearly trespassed. They had clearly, in a technical sense, violated the law by going into a Draft Board. They were acquitted by the jury when they gave testimony about the reasons for doing this, about their strong feelings about the war in Vietnam and the need to bring public attention to what was going on.

So I guess what I'm saying is that the organizations and activities that you're talking about today, relating to Central America, are in keeping with a very long American tradition. At certain critical moments in history there are people who are willing to technically violate the law in order to stand up for fundamental principles of life and liberty; that is central to the American tradition.

Q. Where do these movements come from?

A. Where do the movements come from? You have asked me a very hard question. They start small. They start with individuals getting together in small groups, people who are aroused by what is going on, who become frustrated by the fact that in certain areas of American society and on certain issues the legal channels do not seem to permit the voice of the public to be heard very well. I think this is especially true in the area of foreign policy. To an extent we have democracy in domestic policy; in foreign policy, democracy doesn't really exist. In foreign policy, representative government doesn't count for very much. Foreign policy is made by a handful of advisors around the President and, in general, the courts have stayed out of the area of foreign policy. Congress also generally has gone along with the President. But there are people who feel that democracy should play a role in foreign policy as well as domestic policy, that people should have a voice. In such cases people have gotten together and organized movements of social protest and then the idea has spread.

Q. Outside such organized movements of social protest, as you put it, does an individual have the ability to influence foreign policy?

A. It is very hard, very hard. It is even hard for individual congressmen and senators to influence foreign policy.

I remember talking to a Catholic priest who had engaged in an act of civil disobedience during the Vietnam War. He said he never dreamed of doing such a thing, but he was so anguished by what he saw happening in Vietnam to the American GIs and to the people in Vietnam, all of them suffering in a war which he felt to be needless, that he went up to see Senator Kennedy of Massachusetts. He thought, well, here's a senator of the United States; he's a person with power. And Kennedy told him that he and the Senate and the Congress generally were helpless to do very much about the war; that he, as an individual senator, could not do very much. So in the area of foreign affairs when a policy becomes obviously wrong, destructive of life in another country and in our own country, it is sometimes necessary for citizens to get together and to create democracy. Democracy is not just voting. Democracy is not just writing letters to congressmen. Democracy in America has always meant people getting together, meeting, petitioning, demonstrating, going out in the street; yes, sitting in, trespassing, doing various acts of nonviolent, technical disobedience to arouse large numbers of people.

The slavery issue in 1840 was not a big issue for most of the American people. Between 1850 and 1860, largely as a result of the actions that were taken against the Fugitive Slave Act, the sentiment of the American people was aroused in an enormous way against slavery.

Q. So can you make an overall statement of the success of popular movements in affecting government foreign policy?

A. Well, in the case of the Vietnam War we have a really rare instance in history; not just in American history, but in world history. I guess we should be proud that it happened in our country. That people carried on a whole variety of tactics of popular protest, including civil disobedience, and in the course of several years turned the nation around in its opinion about the war and made the leaders of the country sit up and take notice about what was happening in the public. And they took account. If you read *The Pentagon Papers*, the official history of the war as compiled by the Department of Defense, which the public got to see by an act of civil disobedience, you can see that they took account. In the spring of 1968, the U.S. government had to make the decision whether to give General Westmoreland two hundred thousand more troops. We already had five hundred thousand troops in Vietnam, and he wanted two hundred thousand more. Lyndon Johnson set up this little team. They investigated the situation and they came back to Johnson and they said, you cannot do this. The American people will not stand for it. There has been too much protest, too much draft resistance. The population has been moved against the war to such an extent that we have to begin de-escalating, turning the other way, and begin to curtail the bombing and so on. In the case of Vietnam, it was clear that this movement, which had started with a handful of people who were looked upon as kind of wild for the things they did, had succeeded in affecting the mood and spirit of the majority of the American people by 1969, 1970.

Q. Thank you.

THE COURT: Thank you, Mr. McCullough. Ms. Shingler?

Cross-Examination by MS. SHINGLER:

Q. Good morning, Mr. Zinn.

A. Good morning.

Q. Mr. Zinn, isn't it true that sitting-in is only one form of civil disobedience that can effect change?

A. Oh, yes.

MS. SHINGLER: Thank you. Nothing further.

THE COURT: Mr. McCullough?

Re-Direct Examination by MR. McCULLOUGH:

Q. I just have one question to clarify something you said earlier. You testified it's very difficult for one senator to have any effect. If that's the case, how can civil disobedience, such as we have been talking about all week in this trial, have effect on the foreign policy of the country?

A. Are you talking about civil disobedience in general? The way civil disobedience works is that it affects the public. It affects the majority of the people. It does more than affect one senator. It affects many senators. It affects many congressmen. It affects the President. It affects the military leaders of the country because what a government needs most of all when it carries out its foreign policy is legitimacy. It needs support. The government understands it cannot commit its young men to die in war unless it can build up popular support for that policy. When the people see that a war is being fought for no good reason or that the military aid only has the effect of increasing the violence or of supporting some dictatorial government, and the government sees that such policies have lost their popular support, then the government has to begin to think twice about whether it will continue those policies.

Q. Now, when you refer to the government, the government is actually a collection of individuals, individual senators, individual representatives, right? And so one would have to look at each representative's position to decide whether and how to change their position. Is that how you actually analyze the mechanics?

A. Well, the actual process by which this develops is very complicated, but I think it's fair to say that you hope to affect enough individual senators, enough individual congressmen, enough individual members of the executive branch for there to begin to be a kind of reverberating effect between the legislative branches, the Presidency, and the public, which will result in a change in policy.

MR. McCULLOUGH: Thank you very much.

THE COURT: Thank you very much, Dr. Zinn. I appreciate your coming up, sir.

MATTHEW COUNTRYMAN, being duly affirmed, testified as follows:

Direct Examination by MS. BAIRD:

Q. Good morning. Would you state your name and address for the jury, please?

A. My name is Matthew Countryman. I live in New Haven, Connecticut.

Q. And what is your present occupation, Mr. Countryman?

A. I am currently a student at Yale University.

Q. What was your occupation prior to becoming a student?

A. I was a Legislative Aide for the Friends' Committee on National Legislation in Washington, D.C. from September '83, to July '84.

Q. What did your duties involve?

A. I was primarily responsible for Central America policy.

Q. Would you describe the organization that you were employed by for the jury?

A. Sure. The Friends' Committee is a Quaker lobby organization. It seeks to represent the interest of Quakers and other who follow the same values.

Q. Starting in January, 1984, did you have any specific responsibilities while you were lobbying with the Friends?

A. Yes. I worked with a coalition of religious organizations that had decided to emphasize Central America in their work in Washington. We represented a number of Protestant, Catholic and Jewish denominations, and organizations who felt that the administration's policy in Central America was both ineffective and morally wrong. We worked for a change in that policy by lobbying and informing people throughout the country of what was going on in Central America and in Washington.

Q. Were there any critical votes coming up in March of '84?

A. Yes. In early March, the President requested that the Senate add ninety-three million dollars in military aid to El Salvador and another twenty-one million dollars in covert assistance to the rebels fighting in Nicaragua to an emergency food aid bill that was designed for famine relief in southern Africa.

Q. Can you comment on the strategy that was used in appending those military aid bills to the food assistance bill?

A. Sure. The food assistance bill had been passed by the House in a very quick fashion because the aid was very necessary. They said that if Africans did not receive the aid by the end of the month it would basically be ineffective.

Q. This aid was destined to go where?

A. It was destined to go to countries in southern Africa in areas where the drought, at that point, was most devastating.

Q. Please continue.

A. The House had passed this bill and it had gone to the Senate for action. By asking that the Senate add money, at that point, the President was effectively avoiding a full discussion by all the members of the House. He decided that he would rather attempt to get the Senate to support the bill and then go to what is called a Conference where only a few members of the House would have input into the discussions and negotiations of the bill, and thereby avoid some of the major critics of his policy.

Q. So, in effect, by appending the military aid bill to the food assistance package, a full debate in the House was going to be avoided?

A. Right. And the President also hoped that because the food was so necessary and so urgent, he could force them to take the military aid with a minimum of debate because of the need to get the food aid to Africa.

Q. Can you say more specifically what this military aid was to be used for?

A. The military aid would have provided helicopters, replacement parts, ammunition, and other military supplies to the army in El Salvador for their campaign against the rebels there. Also, the covert assistance would have been . . .

Q. When you say covert assistance . . . ?

A. The CIA has unofficially admitted to operating a covert assistance program against Nicaragua.

Q. Does covert mean the same thing as secret?

A. Yes, it does. This covert assistance program is to the rebel groups that are fighting from Honduras and Costa Rica against the Nicaraguan government. The reason that it's called covert or secret is that when we give foreign military aid we give it to a government and these rebel groups aren't a government, they're paramilitary bands, and so it has to be done secretly through the CIA. President Reagan basically admitted that in the televised debate with Walter Mondale just last month.

Q. Now, did you have a strategy in your lobbying on this issue?

A. We thought that our chances for defeating the President's maneuver were very strong for a number of reasons. People in the House were upset because he was trying to attach it to a food aid bill. In the Senate he attempted to avoid the critical members of the Central Intelligence Committee and the Foreign Relations Committee by going to another committee, and there were people upset about that maneuver as well. But we also felt that the merit of the situation would allow us to defeat this bill. Opposition had grown very strong to covert military aid in the House and the Senate. That meant that if we could get a strong vote in the Senate, not necessarily a victory, it would mean that our chances of defeating it in Conference would be very good.

Q. I can see from our discussion that the lobbying strategy becomes rather complicated. I wonder if you could explain to the jury where Senator Stafford fits into all of this?

A. Okay. The Senate is controlled by the Republicans, the same party as the President. Senator Stafford is a Republican. But Senator Stafford is considered one of about ten to fifteen moderate Republicans who are more independent from the President, who have opposed him on some issues, and who we felt were not sure whether they could support the President on this issue. We did not have hard vote evidence because the Senate had avoided voting on any aspect of Central America policy for over a year and a half. They had never voted on covert assistance against Nicaragua even though it had been going on for three years. So without hard evidence we relied on statements that they made to constituents in newsletters and statements that we had received in our lobbying efforts. We felt that these moderate senators were unsure of their position. They were concerned about the level and effectiveness of military activity in Central America, the putting aside of economic programs, and the fact that if the President decided to send in American troops they would be politically damaged.

Q. Was Senator Stafford one of these moderate senators that you're speaking of?

A. Yes, he was.

Q. And he was a focus of your lobbying?

A. Yes, he was. For five weeks preceding the vote in the first week of April, we lobbied in teams of two or three, visiting a number of moderate Republicans. I personally visited Senator Stafford's aide.

Q. Did you get to see Senator Stafford?

A. No, I did not.

Q. And did you work with the other organizations that we've been hearing about, such as the Committee in Solidarity with the People of El Salvador?

A. Yes, we did. The week of March 19th to the 25th was organized as Central America Week. We were endorsed by over sixty national religious organizations as well as student groups, professional groups, peace groups, liberal political organizations. Tuesday, March 20th was a National Day of Citizen Advocacy where we had people from throughout the country come to Washington to meet with their representatives, to oppose the President's Central America policy.

Q. Was the vote in April a matter of public record?

A. Yes.

Q. Are you aware of what Senator Stafford's vote was?

A. He voted against the aid to the contras.

MS. BAIRD: No further questions.

THE COURT: Mr. Bradley?

MR. BRADLEY: No questions, Your Honor.

THE COURT: Very well. Thank you very much, Mr. Countryman.

GLADIS SANCHEZ, being duly sworn by the Court Officer in English, and translated by the Interpreter, testified as follows:

Direct Examination by MS. BAIRD:

Q. Would you state your name?

A. Gladis Sanchez.

Q. How old are you?

A. Twenty-two.

Q. Where do you live now?

A. Westbury, Long Island.

Q. What do you do in Long Island?

A. I work for the Central America Refugee Committee.

Q. Do you also work for a living for wages?

A. Yes, I clean houses.

Q. How long have you been in the States?

A. Since December, 1981.

Q. Where are you from, Ms. Sanchez?

A. El Salvador.

Q. Where did you live with your family in El Salvador?

A. In the city of Mejicanos.

Q. What did your family do?

A. My mother had a store.

Q. Did you all live together?

A. Yes.

Q. How many people?

A. About twenty.

Q. In one house?

A. Yes.

Q. And who was in your family in that house?

A. My brothers and sisters, and my aunts and uncles from the countryside.

Q. They had all come to live in the city from the country?

A. Yes.

Q. Why did they do that?

A. My immediate family came years ago to look for better living circumstances, but my relatives came because of the current political situation.

Q. What do you mean by a current political situation?

A. Because *la guardia* came to the town where they were living.

Q. What is *la guardia*?

A. They're part of the national armed forces. They would go from house to house searching for arms.

Q. What happened?

A. At first just my family left, but very shortly thereafter there was an air raid or bombardment after which the entire town evacuated the area.

Q. What kind of work did you do in Mejicanos, Ms. Sanchez?

A. I worked with a Christian base community, teaching catechism.

Q. We've heard a lot about Christian base communities. What is that exactly?

A. They are groups that form from the broad Christian community into smaller community action groups whose work consists of addressing various needs such as catechism, reading and writing, and everyday survival. This was organized originally by Monsignor Archbishop Romero.

Q. The Archbishop in El Salvador, is that correct?

A. Yes.

Q. In this Christian base community you taught people to read and write?

A. Yes, we would go out to the marginal zones of these communities and discover that there were eleven and twelve-year-olds who had no reading and writing ability whatsoever, and we would teach them to read and write.

Q. Why did you join this work?

A. It was part of the church effort that has been growing and developing for some time. This catechizing mission, this reading and writing and teaching, this going out, originated in the church.

Q. And these groups also took care sometimes of the material needs of the people; clothing, fuel, things of that nature?

A. Yes, food also.

Q. Did there come a time when the government began to oppose these groups?

A. Yes.

Q. Is there a certain date for that, or was it always present?

A. You could date it from the first assassination of a Catholic priest which occurred in March, 1977.

Q. Was this a priest that you knew, Ms. Sanchez?

A. Yes.

Q. What was he doing to get assassinated?

A. His name was Rutilio Grande. He was doing the same kind of work that Monsignor Romero would do later, which was going to the marginal zones and addressing the needs of people he found there. And he was denouncing the government.

Q. Who assassinated him?

A. Soldiers.

Q. In uniform?

A. Yes.

Q. Were there other examples of government opposition to your group that you remember?

A. In 1978 the priest I was working with was also murdered.

Q. Were friends of yours also kidnapped, or murdered, or tortured?

A. Yes.

Q. Can you describe that?

A. Tony was taken by the police and incarcerated, subjected to electric shock and torture. He was released because he had an uncle in the military. It was he that subsequently came to my house and warned us that we had better be on the alert. And then there was the case of Cecilia.

Q. First of all, who was Tony? Who was Cecilia?

A. Both of them were members of our Christian community.

Q. Who is Cecilia, a friend or relative?

A. We grew up together. We were raised together.

Q. Was she doing the same kind of work that you were doing?

A. Yes, she was.

Q. What happened to her?

A. She disappeared. She was taken from her home. She appeared in some coffee plantation, her face covered with acid. She had no breasts and she had a stake in her vagina.

Q. Ms. Sanchez, did there come a time when you were worried about your own safety?

A. Yes, I received a threatening letter.

Q. What did that letter say?

A. The church is a center of subversion and communism.

Q. The church meaning your Christian base community or the Catholic Church?

A. They sent it to the church I was working at because they considered the church subversive and communistic. People who have been displaced from their zones, who encountered trouble of some kind, would tell their pastors about it. If the pastor then publicly, or in mass, denounces practices like this, he goes under suspicion and is considered dangerous or subversive.

Q. Pastor of the church?

A. Yes.

Q. Was there anything else in this letter?

A. That anyone belonging to this subversive church must pay with their lives.

Q. Was that the only threat that you received?

A. No. My mother's store was later burned down.

Q. What year was that?

A. In 1980.

Q. Did you leave your home at that time?

A. No, we stayed in the house.

Q. Did anything else happen after that that led you to believe you were in danger?

A. Yes; on the door of my house appeared the "white hand."

Q. What is the "white hand?"

A. It's the symbol or sign of the death squads, when they wish to threaten.

Q. How do you know that they come from the death squads? How do you know, Ms. Sanchez?

A. There are many cases for a long time now. The death squad sign, be it on a home, on a store, on a church, or at a school, has been to leave the "white hand."

Q. People know that it comes from death squads?

A. Yes, because they also leave written words.

Q. After you received this "white hand" sign did you leave El Salvador?

A. Yes.

Q. Is your family still in El Salvador?

A. Yes.

Q. What has happened to them since you left?

A. A cousin who came to live in California has told me that my brother disappeared, but then reappeared. And that an uncle of mine has been killed and turned up under a bridge.

MS. BAIRD: Thank you very much.

THE COURT: Thank you, Ms. Baird. Ms. Shingler?

MS. SHINGLER: No questions.

THE COURT: Thank you very much.

RICHARD FALK, having been duly sworn to tell the truth, the whole truth and nothing but the truth, testified as follows:

Direct Examination by MS. VANCE:

Q. Would you state your name and address, please?

A. Richard Anderson Falk, Princeton, New Jersey.

Q. What is your current occupation?

A. I'm a professor of International Law and Practice at Princeton University.

Q. Professor Falk, could you tell us your educational background, please?

A. I have a Bachelor of Science and Economics degree from the University of Pennsylvania in 1952, a law degree from Yale Law School in 1955, and a Doctoral degree from Harvard in 1962.

Q. Are you connected with any organizations that focus on foreign relations or foreign policy?

A. Yes. Two professional ones that I am connected with are the National Studies Association and the Council on Foreign Relations.

Q. Do you ever consult with Congressional bodies on matters of foreign relations and foreign policy?

A. I have testified as an expert witness on a number of occasions before Senate and House committees, including the Senate Committee on Foreign Relations and House Committee on Foreign Affairs.

Q. What are your specific areas of interest in terms of foreign policy and foreign relations at the moment?

A. I have been particularly interested recently in the relationship between political democracy, public opinion, and the formation of foreign policy. I have also been interested in the role of force in international affairs and the relevance of law and morality to the use of force. And I have been concerned with national security policy, the nuclear arms race, and international institutions that relate to these kinds of issues.

Q. I wonder if you could tell us a little bit about your research and findings on the first of those interests, the relationship between foreign policy and political democracy. Could you explain to the jury the concepts behind that relationship?

A. I think that one of the things that's most important about our particular system of government is that it relies on citizens and their initiatives to be sure that the government doesn't exceed its legal and constitutional boundaries. Throughout our history as a country the role of direct action by citizens has played an enormous part, generally a constructive part, in shaping the behavior of Congress, of the President, of the media. We are a democracy in which the basic idea is that the government should serve the people and that the people have a responsibility to make sure that the government doesn't exceed its constitutional functions. And I think, particularly in the period since the end of World War II, a very important series of developments has made this more important than ever before.

Earlier in our history, except during times of war, we basically were demobilized and did not have a strong, permanent military establishment that was part of the governing process. Since World War II, partly because of our global role, partly because of the nature of nuclear weapons and the fact that war is never very far away, we have built up a permanent military presence within the government. And this has changed and, to some degree, distorted the way in which the constitutional functions of government have been carried out.

It was always felt by the people that established the constitution that it was very risky to have standing armies and there was a great debate about whether we could avoid becoming a military society if we established standing armies that would exist even during peace time. Now we have become so accustomed to having a permanently strong military presence in our government, with all the secrecy and the surveillance and the erosion of civil liberties that this involves, that we no longer are sufficiently sensitive to the degree to which the military now dominates Congress and the media in a way that distorts the formation of policy. I think direct action by citizens and peace groups and religious organizations plays an even more vital role than before in checking the abuse of governmental power.

Q. Professor Falk, can you give us some specific examples of citizen acts that have affected the conduct of U.S. foreign policy?

A. I think the most important recent example would be the role of the peace movement in relation to the conduct and continuation of the Vietnam War. I think that citizen actions, peaceful demonstrations and the like, had an enormous effect on the way Congress eventually perceived the war and how the leadership in the White House carried on and perceived the war. There is considerable evidence now on the basis of declassified documents that had the peace movement not existed the U.S. government very likely would have waged a systematic bombing campaign against the dike system in North Vietnam, conceivably causing the death of two or three million civilians. This was, I think, effectively inhibited by public opinion. The Swedish Ambassador played a role, but also a very important role was played by citizens with no formal governmental status.

Another important example has been our relationship to South Africa, where I think groups of citizens of all kinds have made it more possible for the government to put direct pressure on South Africa with respect to its racial policies. This has taken the form of restricting the kinds of employment practices that U.S. corporations are able to follow in South Africa. It has led to an export ban on weapons to South Africa, and a number of other things which I think there is reason to believe the government wouldn't have done without that kind of public pressure.

I should add that the U.S. government is not carrying out this popular mandate in a constructive way. I think it would certainly promote the goal of greater human rights for the people of South Africa if there was more public pressure on this issue.

Q. Professor Falk, can you think of examples of any other countries that have changed their human rights or foreign relations policy as a result of public pressure at home?

A. Yes. I think that a good example would be the conduct by France of its war against the Algerian Independence Movement in the 1950s. Between 1954 and 1962 there was widespread evidence that the French were relying on systematic torture to break the will of the Algerian nationalists' movement. As a consequence of a very strong public campaign in France, by French citizens, there was substantial abandonment of those practices by the government.

I think, also, British Colonial policy was affected to a considerable degree by public pressure in England. I believe that the process of achieving independence for India would have been longer and bloodier had not the citizen actions taken place.

Q. Professor Falk, based on other situations that you've studied, can public pressure at home have any effect on U.S. conduct in Central America?

A. Yes, I think there is no question that it can have an effect on the general attitude of the public, of the media, of our elected representatives in Congress, and of the White House. I think it can have an effect even on how courts and juries perceive the concerns of the community. I think it can generally be of tremendous help in clarifying what the people of this country believe is the right thing to do in foreign affairs. If I'm correct that our system of government stands for the fundamental idea that it is the will of the people that should ultimately be expressed in official policies, then it seems to me it is extremely important to give every opportunity for the people to be able to express their concern about the immoral and illegal implications of our foreign policy towards Central America, which I think unquestionably exist at the present time.

MS. VANCE: Thank you very much, Professor Falk. I have no more questions.

THE COURT: Mr. Bradley?

MR. BRADLEY: Thank you, Your Honor.

Cross-Examination by MR. BRADLEY:

Q. Professor Falk, with respect to the types of things that citizens can do, demonstrations or sit-ins, can you tell us what other types of activities the populace could get involved in that can affect American policy, affect their senator or congressman?

A. Well, I think that we have a very rich tradition of possible initiatives. One of the most important ones, even though it's been very selectively used throughout our history, is the various forms of civil disobedience, symbolic violations of the law, in order to promote visions of justice, visions of legality that appear to be jeopardized by the kind of policies that the government is pursuing. I think the United States is admired throughout the world for this tradition of civil disobedience as much as for any other feature of our political life.

Q. In addition to civil disobedience, what else can one do?

A. Well, I'm not sure of the full range of what you mean. Obviously, there are all the forms of political activity including seeking to alter the composition of electoral bodies, political platforms, political education of a variety of forms — all sorts of things that we associate with citizen participation in democracy.

Q. Is it fair to say, then, that civil disobedience is not the only alternative that one has to try to influence their government officials?

A. It's certainly fair to say that. On the other hand, in a given context of urgency where people are being killed and where risk of war exists, I think symbolic nonviolent acts of civil disobedience are extremely appropriate.

Q. Appropriate, but not the only alternative.

A. Perhaps not the only alternative, but given the —

Q. Thank you, Professor Falk.

A. — policies of government, perhaps the only effective alternative.

MR. BRADLEY: No other questions, Your Honor.

THE COURT: Very well; Ms. Vance?

MS. VANCE: No more questions.

THE COURT: Thank you very much, Professor Falk.

At the Court's request, Professor Falk testified further on international law as it relates to U.S. policy toward Central America. This testimony was taken in the judge's chambers and is reproduced in its entirety as an Appendix.

MR. McGILL: Your Honor, the defense calls the Honorable Ramsey Clark.

RAMSEY CLARK, after being duly sworn by the Court to tell the truth, the whole truth and nothing but the truth, testified as follows:

Direct Examination by MR. McGILL:

Q. Would you state your name and address, please, sir?

A. Ramsey Clark, New York.

Q. And what is your occupation?

A. I'm a lawyer.

Q. Could you briefly outline for the jury your professional training and experience?

A. I went to law school one year at the University of Texas and then I transferred to the University of Chicago. I graduated from there a long time ago, in 1950. I went back home to Texas and practiced law down there for about nine years. Then I went to Washington at the beginning of the Kennedy administration and served in the Department of Justice for the eight years of the Kennedy/Johnson administration, from January, '61, to January of '69. Then I took off for about a year and wrote a book and did other things because I didn't think a former Attorney General should be meddling for a while.

Q. I take it, then, that part of your term with the Justice Department was as Attorney General of the United States?

A. That's right. I was an Assistant Attorney General, and then Deputy Attorney General, and then the Attorney General. I've practiced law since then. My office is in New York, but I don't get to visit it very often.

Q. While you were the Attorney General of the United States, did part of your function require you to familiarize yourself with the United States Constitution and laws?

A. I thought so.

Q. Have you made a study of the right to petition?

A. I have, yes. I studied it over a long period of time. I authored the entry on the right to petition and to assembly in the *Dictionary of American History*.

Q. While you were Attorney General of the United States, did you have occasion to prosecute or order the prosecution of persons involved in sit-ins or similar kinds of activities which were designed to effect changes in government policy?

A. Well, I was there all through the '60s, and the major issue of those years was civil rights, which involved marches and demonstrations and sit-ins and things. Towards the end of that time the war in Vietnam also provoked similar activities which we had to address. There were numerous types of cases and many more actual cases involving what you could call protests against government policies.

Q. Since you resumed private practice have you defended cases of protest activity against government policy?

A. Yes, I have, pretty consistently.

Q. Is there a distinction to be drawn between activity directed in an effort to communicate with an elected representative and activity say at a nuclear power plant?

A. Well, I think there is. The Constitution gives you the right to petition. It's a right that was developed at great price over many years. Most say it began with the Magna Carta, but even in the Magna Carta a person had to appeal to four out of twenty-five barons, and if he had the courage to do that and didn't get —

MR. BRADLEY: Objection, Your Honor. With all due respect to Mr. Clark and his knowledge of the law, the law should come from the Court and not from the witness.

MR. McGILL: Your Honor, I believe he is testifying as to the history of something which is now the law and on which the Court will charge the jury. This goes to the background and the importance of the structure and function of government, not to what the law now is.

THE COURT: Yes, I think some incidental reference to law is probably necessary for Mr. Clark. However, I'm sure the jury understands that the law that is to apply in this case will come from the Court at the end of the case. Go ahead, Mr. McGill.

MR. McGILL: Thank you, Your Honor.

Q. Could you please describe for us how the right of petition developed?

A. The Magna Carta set up the first opportunity for the public, through the barons, to address the king about grievances. The idea of the parliament representing the people came from that. There had to be this representation. It was the English Bill of Rights of 1689 that first prohibited the king from punishing people for trying to complain to him about something in their lives that hurt. And then, of course, it's Article I in our Constitution that you have this right to petition government. It's the only way that representative government can work, that the people have a chance to say to their representatives what it is that troubles them.

Q. How important is it to a representative government that people exercise their right to petition?

A. Well, representative government can't function without it. That's the way that the representative knows from her constituents what it is they want their government to do.

Q. Why should citizens be allowed to participate in decisions relating to foreign policy?

A. It's their children that get sent off to war and get killed, among other things.

Q. In order for citizens to participate is it necessary for them to have accurate information?

A. Of course. That's basic to the whole idea of democracy and the hope for meaningful republican government and the possibility of peace.

Q. How does it affect the representatives in a democracy when misinformation is promulgated by agencies of government itself?

A. Well, it destroys the chance for truth and reason to guide government and human conduct.

Q. From your experience do you have an opinion as to whether the exercise of the right of petition does have an impact on government conduct?

A. It has an enormous impact; absolutely.

Q. Can you give us an example?

A. Well, anyone who's ever worked with a legislative body, such as the U.S. Congress, realizes how dramatically powerful the opinion of the constituents, meaningfully communicated, is, in how they vote. They have to go home and run for office again some day.

Q. Have you ever been to Central America?

A. I have been there many times going back to 1946. I have been there probably a dozen times in the last two and a half years.

Q. Have you been to El Salvador and Nicaragua?

A. I have been to both those countries on numerous occasions in the last several years.

Q. Are you familiar with American policy there, and what effect it's had on people in the region?

A. Sadly, I am.

Q. In view of your knowledge of Central America and on the functioning of representative government, do you have an opinion as to whether there needs to be some communication by the people with their elected representatives about U.S. government policy in Central America?

A. Well, I think there always needs to be that. I think the people always need to be involved, but if the people want peace, if they don't want their government committing crimes in their name, they have to learn and speak out on these issues. And of all the areas of concern in the world today, the policies of our government in Central America are among the most urgent.

MR. McGILL: Thank you. I have no further questions, Your Honor.

THE COURT: Thank you, Mr. McGill. Mr. Bradley?

MR. BRADLEY: No questions, Your Honor.

THE COURT: I appreciate your coming up, sir.

MR. DORSCH: Defense calls Jeanne Keller.

JEANNE KELLER, being duly affirmed, testified as follows:

Direct Examination by MR. DORSCH:

Q. You are Jeanne Keller?

A. Yes, I am Jeanne Keller.

Q. And you live in Burlington, Vermont?

A. Yes, sir.

Q. And you are employed in Burlington?

A. Yes, I am.

Q. Can you tell the jury how you came to be one of the Defendants?

A. The long version or the short version?

Q. Well, I want to get home tonight. Why don't we do the short version.

A. Well, I was in Senator Stafford's office over the weekend in question. I think what brought me there, really, is that I was raised in a politically-aware family, a conservative Republican family. My father encouraged us to pay attention to what was going on in current events. That was what we discussed at the dinner table. He quizzed us on *Weekly Reader* kinds of things. So I grew up with the sense of the importance of being aware of different events that affected us as citizens. He was a state representative. So I took a great interest in politics because of that. I have always been interested in politics.

Q. Were you there to petition or have some influence on Senator Stafford?

A. Yes.

Q. Now, I don't want to get into the long version, but when you reached the decision to be involved in whatever happened over the weekend of March 26th, did you have occasion to speak to the people who ultimately became your co-Defendants?

A. Yes, we had incredibly long meetings. That's the long version.

Q. Now, you said that you were brought up in a family that was oriented toward public affairs. Can you tell us what kinds of professional experiences you have had that would relate to public affairs?

A. Well, I was student body president in high school.

Q. That's very admirable.

Q. Thank you. I have worked on people's campaigns, that kind of thing. I put my first bumper sticker on when I was twelve years old.

Q. And who was that for, your father?

A. Yes, that was for my father. But as I grew up and became an adult, I started thinking about my own political beliefs, working for candidates and lobbying. I really enjoyed lobbying. In fact, I spent some time in Washington lobbying.

Q. Have you ever held any government positions?

A. Yes.

Q. And in the course of holding those government positions did you reach any conclusions about the effect of public petitioning on government officials?

A. Absolutely. That is the way that a government official who wants to be responsive to the citizens can know about what is going on. They can read it in the paper, but the best way is to hear it from the citizens.

Q. Now, did your experience as a government official lead to your decision to be involved in the events of the March 26th weekend?

A. In some ways I wanted to be a government official because I wanted to be responsive to citizens, and having been a government official also made me feel that it was important to contact other government officials.

Q. Before we started this trial, I believe you told me that you had had some direct connection with Senator Stafford about an issue other than Central America.

A. Yes. About two years ago I worked with a group of people who formed an organization called the Vermont Coalition on Acid Rain. The Clean Air Act was coming up before Congress so we drew together a number of organizations, the Lung Association and some other health and lobbying organizations, to work on that issue. Senator Stafford was a key person on that bill.

Q. Is that an area of particular interest to him?

A. Yes, he is on a very important committee, Environment and Public Works.

Q. Did you have occasion to speak to him and meet with him?

A. Yes, we did.

Q. Can you tell the jury what was discussed and what your impression was of the Senator's interest and appreciation?

A. He was extremely responsive on the issue of acid rain. He was especially concerned that the people in Vermont were paying a price in damage to our environment so that people in the Midwest could have lower electric rates and he didn't think that was fair. He thought that was an injustice and that it was up to the federal government to do something about it. Since it was something that the administration differed from him on, he told us it was critical that we get as many people out in support of him on this issue as we could, because he could then go to Washington and say, look, I have all these people back in Vermont who are really fired up, who really are concerned about acid rain. I'm representing them, and something has to be done.

Q. Now, that was the current administration you're talking about?

A. Yes, that was the Reagan administration.

Q. So he indicated to you that he would be willing, in certain circumstances, to lobby and vote against the Reagan administration?

A. Well, he out-and-out thought that their position was not good on this issue.

Q. Did he encourage further contact with you or your organization?

A. Yes. In fact, our organization worked with his staff on a public hearing on acid rain. We worked to get as many people there as we could; the idea being that a big turnout at a meeting like that would show public support for his controversial stand against the Reagan administration.

Q. Did he express his appreciation of that hearing afterwards?

A. Over and over and over.

Q. Did anything else happen with him with respect to the acid rain issue?

A. Well, we continued to work with him through that term of Congress and ended up getting some of what we wanted and we were successful in forestalling efforts to just eliminate the Clean Air Act altogether. He always made it clear that he was grateful for what we had done to support him because the White House was really giving him a hard time.

Q. Was the Senator influential in the positions taken by Congress on this issue?

A. Yes. It wasn't just because he was chair of that committee; it was also that he was a ranking Republican in the Senate and he was thought of as being very deliberate and very careful about the decisions he made. So when he turned on the issue of acid rain he brought a lot of people with him just because of who he is and the way that the Senate operates.

Q. Based upon your experience with the Senator on acid rain and environmental issues, did you come away with an impression of what kind of a Senator was representing us down in Washington? Was he responsive?

A. Yes. I was really pleased because of the cooperation we had from his staff, and also the gratitude that he showed to us. We had a luncheon where we honored him for the work that he had done, and he said this really should be a luncheon to honor us. A lot of politicians don't do that, you know.

Q. Did he at any time indicate his interest was solely on environmental issues and that you should limit your petitions or your information to him to those issues?

A. Not at that time.

Q. Now, there came a time when your concerns and attentions focused on Central America?

A. Yes.

Q. When your attention focused on Central America, did you undertake any conversations with Senator Stafford on that issue?

A. Yes.

Q. How often, in your recollection, did that happen?

A. Oh, I don't know. I sent him telegrams. I wrote letters. I made phone calls.

Q. How many times?

A. Many times.

Q. And what, if any, response did you get from the Senator?

A. Well, for one thing, I was never able to even talk with any of the Senator's staff. The message would be taken by the receptionist who answered the phone. They would take my name and thank me for calling. The staff members were never available to discuss Central America.

Q. And that was in spite of the fact that you had had personal contact with the Senator's staff and with the Senator in the past?

A. Yes.

Q. Did the Senator at any time indicate his knowledge of, or interest in, Central American issues?

A. Well, I received the same form letters that the other Defendants talked about. It would say that he is not on a committee with jurisdiction for this issue, so it really isn't something that he knows a lot about, and he thanked me for writing.

Q. Have you ever been successful in getting a response from Senator Stafford, or even his staff, on Central America?

A. I was getting form letters back that didn't answer my questions. I would write a letter, and I would write another letter. These are the questions. Please just answer these questions. And I didn't feel that they were being answered.

Q. Have you had the occasion to go to Nicaragua or go to El Salvador?

A. No.

Q. Why have you not?

A. Well, I really can't afford to leave my job and my family.

Q. Are you aware of some of your co-Defendants who have gone?

A. Yes. Through some of the people who had gone on the Witness for Peace program I was able to learn some things I didn't know because I'm not able to go. You know, not everybody can go.

Q. To your knowledge, have the Witness for Peace actions changed the United States policy in Central America?

A. I think for a temporary amount of time, they will change the way the army acts. They will save lives while they're there, maybe. But, you know, in the larger picture you have to prevent the army from having the guns. Why should American citizens have to go down to a foreign country to stop our tax money from killing people? Why don't we just change it up here? That is my feeling.

Q. Focusing again on the period of time before the weekend of March 26th, to your knowledge, did Senator Stafford's position change in any way as a result of the Witness for Peace actions?

A. Well, I knew from talking with Witness participants who had come back that they were having trouble getting to him.

Q. Have you or your co-Defendants telephoned the Senator's office?

A. Oh, that's the minimum of what we did. That was just the beginning.

Q. And to your knowledge, have those phone calls met with success or satisfactory responses?

A. No, ma'am.

Q. Let's go on to the letter writing. Have you or your co-Defendants written letters?

A. Yes.

Q. And to your knowledge, have the letters changed anything?

A. No, we're getting the same form letter back.

Q. What about telegrams?

A. Yes, we have sent telegrams.

Q. Has that changed anything?

A. No.

Q. Now, subsequent to March 26th, do you have any opinion as to whether your activities at his office had an effect on the Senator?

A. Yes.

Q. Can you tell the jury what that is?

A. Well, I think it's interesting that during the amendment process leading to the vote on contra funding, Senator Stafford was not present for a key vote. From my work in Washington as a lobbyist I know that that is a form of backing off on a position. I call it taking a walk, because if you're in town and you don't show up for a roll call vote, it's a deliberate act. It's called taking a walk, and it's an honorable thing to do. In fact, it's respected. It's often what you try to get a person to do. You try to get someone who hasn't made up their mind yet to at least take a walk.

Q. As we know, Senator Stafford has a hip replacement, but he's been walking recently?

A. Yes.

Q. How has he been walking?

A. Very well.

Q. That's your personal opinion?

A. Well, I saw him walking into a public meeting and that's the next effect I think we had. He did, in fact, end up having the kind of public meeting that we had been asking for. At that public meeting, he said he had heard a lot of things that he never heard before that were very disturbing and troubling, and that he was going to try as much as was humanly possible to make sense of it and deliberate on it when he went back to Washington. I believe that he genuinely meant that; that he was made aware of things that had never gotten to him before.

Q. Did his votes in the Congress change subsequent to March 26th?

A. Yes. He very proudly told us at the public meeting that he had voted against aid to the contras.

Q. Do you feel that your actions and the actions of your co-Defendants in any way influenced him to make those changes?

A. Yes, I do.

Q. Now, I believe the testimony has been that you were in the Senator's office over that weekend with permission, is that correct?

A. Yes. When Mr. Post left, he said "You're welcome to stay."

Q. During the time you were there, did you intend any disrespect of the Senator's authority?

A. No, we were there because of his authority. We were there because he was our elected representative and was really the only person who could do something. I've grown up believing that that's what you do; you go to your elected representative. That's why you elect them, to represent you.

Q. I believe there was earlier testimony that at some point one of the police officers indicated that there was a problem with you staying in the office because there were people who were having a problem with the government and they needed to talk to the Senator's staff.

A. Oh, yes. I thought it was particularly ironic that when Mr. Post told us that it was time to go it was eleven-thirty or so in the morning, which were office hours. He said you will have to leave now, there are people who have problems with the federal government. And I raised my hand and I said I have a problem with the federal government.

Q. There came a time when you knew that there was a possibility that you might be arrested and prosecuted if you continued to stay; is that correct?

A. Yes.

Q. At that time did you have an opinion as to whether or not you had legal authority to be there?

A. Right up to the moment that they came in to take me out, I didn't believe they were going to do it. We were there out of a very basic fundamental obligation that we felt as citizens to make sure that our elected representative knew the consequences of his votes. He had said, well, I don't know much about Central America because I'm not on the committee, but he was still voting and he was still responsible to represent the people and uphold the Constitution. Now, the idea that he would say you have to leave, this place is for people who have problems with the federal government, really underscores a lot of my feelings that day. It was as though it wasn't just his office that they wanted to make off limits, it was also the issue of Central America that was somehow off limits. We were there because it was the only way we had to get to him, and it was really important. We had tried everything. We had written letters. We had made phone calls. We had sent telegrams. Little groups of people had met with him.

We talked at one of those meetings, those interminable meetings, about what that public meeting would be like. We discussed it and what we wanted to have was a debate. We would have the people who supported the administration's policies and we would have people who opposed the administration's policies. It wasn't just going to be a free-for-all, because we were very respectful of him in that way. We didn't want to just put him up there to be barraged. We wanted him to witness a debate because it seemed to us that if four people went and talked to him it wouldn't be as clear as if we had a debate where we would invite someone supporting the policies. We wanted to let him hear the administration's position refuted, to let him hear the arguments right there. Obviously, we weren't able to go down to

Washington and stage a debate with the Secretary of Defense, so that's why it had to be a public meeting. We didn't want to give him limited information. We wanted him to see the whole picture and be able to judge what was reasonable.

Q. During this trial the jury has heard a lot of testimony from various experts and various people who have been in Central America. Are you asking them to consider that testimony and to consider if there was an emergency and that therefore there was a necessity for you to be in Senator Stafford's office?

A. The reason that the testimony is important to me is because it tells exactly why I was there. Every witness that has appeared has made me feel very confident about my right to be there because they are saying what was going through my mind. They are talking about the things that I grew up believing. They're telling the things that I found out about, over the past couple of years, from knowing people who had been to Central America. So their testimony is absolutely essential to understanding why we had to go there, and why we stayed, and why the senator's so important to talk to.

Q. Now, in saying what you just said, are you speaking on behalf of the Defendants as a group?

A. Yes, I am.

Q. Jeanne, Senator Stafford is one vote in the United States Senate. From your personal experience and your professional experience, do you believe one vote matters in a legislative body?

A. Well, my father, who is a state representative, changed his vote on a key issue and the whole thing moved. The whole thing moved. A senator is no different from us, you know. If someone you respect changes his mind, it influences you. It isn't just that they have changed their mind; you think, isn't that interesting? My father was very proud of the fact that when he changed, it changed the course of the legislature. Senator Stafford said that the reason he was such a target for the White House on the acid rain issue was because the White House knew that if he, as a respected Republican senator, took a stand against the administration, then the whole policy might start to crumble.

Q. Was it your opinion that he might have the same effect on Central American policy?

A. I felt, and I still do, that it could be even greater. Of course Vermont is one of the victims of acid rain, but if a Republican senator from Vermont takes an interest in and concern in the lives that are being lost in Central America that is very significant. It's not just one vote then. It changes the whole fabric. It changes the way people look at things.

MR. DORSCH: Nothing further.

THE COURT: Thank you, Mr. Dorsch. Ms. Shingler?

MS. SHINGLER: No questions, Your Honor.

THE COURT: Thank you very much, Ms. Keller. How many more witnesses, Mr. Dorsch?

MR. DORSCH: The Defense rests, Your Honor.

Closing Arguments

For the State of Vermont:

MR. BRADLEY: Good afternoon, ladies and gentlemen. As Judge Mahady explained late this morning, the evidence in this case is now closed. Anything you hear from this point on is the lawyers speaking to you, it is not evidence. What is the evidence in this case is what you remember. It's not what I remember the witnesses saying, and it's not what any of the Defense attorneys remember the witnesses saying. It's only what you remember they said, and it's based on that you must find, ultimately, what the facts in this case are. What the law is in this case will be explained to you by Judge Mahady after the lawyers get through with what are known as our closing arguments. This is our final attempt to try to convince you of the merits of our respective cases.

Now, over the next few minutes I am going to try to explain to you why we feel that you should find that the Defendants in this case are guilty of the crime of unlawful trespass. Over the last few days we have heard quite a bit of testimony about what has gone on in Central America, in the different countries that have been pointed out by many of the witnesses.

What I'd like to remind you is why we are here today. What is it that has brought all of you, all of us, and all of the people here in the courtroom today? It is not the United States policy that has been on trial here, ladies and gentlemen. It is the twenty-six Defendants that are sitting here in the courtroom. It is not, although it is very interesting and I am sure it has been enlightening to you as it has been to me, it is not what is happening here that's important. It's what happened on March 26th of this year that is the crucial element of this case. And what happened, ladies and gentlemen, is that these twenty-six Defendants committed the crime of unlawful trespass.

Now, what is unlawful trespass? What is it here in Vermont? Well, as you recall when we first began here four days ago, Judge Mahady gave you a brief outline of what the crime of unlawful trespass is. What it is that the State has alleged, is that these twenty-six Defendants here in the courtroom today were persons who, without lawful authority, remained upon premises to which they had been given notice of trespass by either the person in charge of the premises, or by a law enforcement officer acting on his behalf. Now, in order for you to come back with a charge of guilty, you must find that the State has proven all of the elements of that offense beyond a reasonable doubt. If you find that we have failed to prove any of those elements beyond a reasonable doubt, then you must return a verdict of not guilty, and you should return a verdict of not guilty. It is our burden to prove otherwise, and it is a burden that the State willingly accepts.

Now, let's look at those elements and let's look back at the testimony that we have heard over the first couple of days of the trial.

Mr. Bradley repeated to the jury the sequence of events of March 23rd-26th.

Now, ladies and gentlemen, I submit to you that a clearer case of unlawful trespass is not going to be found. Warning after warning after warning was given to the people inside, that they were now being asked to leave. They had been there for over seventy hours. Senator Stafford, Mr. Post, and Mr. Pecor had done everything they could do to try and accommodate the protesters in their wish to bring a point across to the people of the State of Vermont and to Senator Stafford. But time had come to get back to business and the protesters refused to leave.

It is unreasonable to think that simply because they were taxpayers that they had a right to be there; because they pay taxes does not give them an unalienable right to take over a public official's office space.

Four people told them that they had to leave. One of them was, for all practical purposes, the person in charge of that office complex. Two of them were uniformed police officers, and yet they remained. They were persons who remained upon the premises to which notices of trespass had been given, having no legal right to do so, and having been asked to leave by the person in lawful possession, or in this case by a law enforcement officer acting on their behalf.

You are not going to ever see a clearer case of unlawful trespass, and I submit to you that on the evidence the State has presented, you will have to find that beyond a reasonable doubt the State has proved all of the elements of that offense. The Defendants were not satisfied with anything that Senator Stafford had said to them and, because they didn't get exactly what they wanted, when they wanted it, despite Senator Stafford's concession that he would now be willing to meet with a few of them, that was not good enough. They didn't get what they wanted so Senator Stafford wasn't going to get his office back. If you're not going to play by my rules then I'm taking my football and going home. It's the same thing, ladies and gentlemen.

Now, over the last several days you have also heard quite a bit of testimony from the Defendants and from their witnesses, as to atrocities, death, and destruction that is going on in Central America. No one in this courtroom is going to deny that. No one here is going to say that the people and the Defendants in this courtroom are wrong and are bad people, but the point is that it is not a situation where a necessity defense should even apply. It is not the type of case where the necessity defense, which in many cases is a valid defense in Vermont, should be invoked or be allowed to absolve the Defendants, in this particular case, from any sort of guilt.

Necessity defense, as I say, is one that does have a valid place in Vermont law and in Vermont history it goes back many, many years, hundreds of years. The common example of a necessity defense is where someone breaks a law in order to prohibit a greater harm. An example of it is where a passerby is walking along and he sees a building on fire and there is another person caught inside the building who is unable to leave, and the passerby has the ability get that person out. Well, it's not his building. He can't simply go running into someone else's building. That may be a trespass. However, the law says that if the passerby goes in under certain circumstances that he may not be committing a criminal offense, or if he is committing a criminal offense he is absolved from it by virtue of the necessity defense.

Necessity defense has four basic elements: first, the harm or the injury that the person is seeking to stop from occurring must have started without any fault on the part of the actor. So in this particular case, the passerby, as long as he did not light the fire or cause the building to burn, would meet that element of the offense.

The second element of the necessity defense is that the harm about to occur is so imminent and so compelling that it is reasonable for the actor to assume that if he does not do anything some great harm is actually going to occur either to himself or to the person he is trying to save. That's the second element.

The third element of the necessity defense is that there can be no other reasonable thing to do in the circumstances. If, in this particular example, there was a fire alarm box on the corner or the burning building was next to the fire station, then there would be something else more reasonable a passerby could do than running into a burning building. He should notify the firemen.

The last element of the necessity defense is that the harm which you're seeking to prohibit is greater than the crime which you're going to have to commit in order to seek to prohibit it. Those are basically the four elements of the necessity defense which has been raised over the last few days by the Defendants.

I would like to address each of those elements now, and to show you why the State feels that under the facts in this case, the necessity defense should not be applied.

First, as I said, the first element of necessity defense is that the harm that you see is not something that you have caused. Most certainly in this case the harm of which we speak, of which the Defendants are speaking, the death and destruction and all the atrocities and the indignities that the people are having in Central America, certainly cannot be said to have been the fault of any of the Defendants here in the courtroom today. The war in Central America has been going on in several places for at least twenty years; in some cases, more than that.

The Defendants' witnesses, who are eminently qualified in many respects, told you about having visited there, told you that the war there has been going on for many, many years. That is the reason why we would suggest that there was not an emergency. What was going on there is horrible. None of us would want to be involved in a war zone like it, but it has in fact been going on for years and years, and with the way things look and the way things are in Central America, it's probably going to go on for many more years, regardless of whether the United States is involved there or not. There is no real emergency. In fact, what the people in Senator Stafford's office were demanding, what their emergency was, was a public meeting called by Senator Stafford. That was their emergency, and not now but soon, sometime within the next few weeks; that was what they wanted. There was no evidence presented that that demonstration at eleven o'clock, March 26th, did anything to save anyone's life in Central America.

Now, certainly in all likelihood, things were going on in El Salvador and Nicaragua at that time, but there has been no evidence presented by the Defendants that they knew exactly what was going on at that time, and there was no clear emergency such as the burning building and the person inside. They were trying to exert some influence on Senator Stafford so that he could exert some influence on other members of the Senate, so that the Senate could take some other action and overcome the administration's policies in Central America. It was going to take quite a bit of time. It was not going to happen right then and there. It was not an emergency.

The second element of the necessity defense is very closely analogous to what I was just saying, and that is that the danger is imminent and compelling. Again, nobody is going to say that a war going on and people being killed is not a tragedy. The question is, in Winooski, Vermont, is a sit-in demonstration in Senator Stafford's office likely to have an immediate effect on what is going on in Nicaragua and El Salvador? And I think you can say to yourself, well, it might have some effect in the future, if everything goes right and if all of the other elements fall into place, yes, it might have an effect. But the question that you have to ask if you are going to look at necessity defense and apply it, is it so imminent, so compelling right now? Is that person about to get burned, and do I have to rush into the building? Was the situation in Central America so imminent and so compelling that the demonstration by the forty-four people in Winooski was necessary right then and there at eleven-thirty a.m. on March 26th? And I suggest to you that it was not. It was too far removed. The emergency was not there.

The third element of the necessity defense is that there can be no reasonable alternative for the actor to take in order to stop the impending harm, and in this case there has been a lot of testimony from the Defendants' witnesses as to what types of things one can do in order to influence the Senator; one of which is to take over his office. You can also write letters. You can also phone. You can have lobbying groups. You can educate the public. You can put up your own candidate. You can raise money to get lobbyists to fight against the senator's policies in Washington. You can go to Washington where you know the Senator is and demonstrate in his office there. You can go to the Oval Office and demonstrate there. There are many different things that one can do. And the crux of the necessity defense is that there is no other thing you can do; that there is only one choice of action that you can take. It doesn't matter if you were frustrated, if you have written letters and you have gotten form letters back. That's the way that our government works. You obviously can write all the letters you want to a senator and a representative. The question for the necessity defense is, was there anything else that they could have done? If the answer to that question is yes, then that element is simply not there. And if one of the elements to the necessity defense is missing, then the entire defense must fail.

The last element to the necessity defense is that the harm, or that which you are doing, outweighs the criminal act which you are being forced to commit. And there is no way to argue that a war is less important than a criminal trespass. But I think if you are thinking that way, perhaps you are looking at it from the wrong direction and you have to begin looking at it from: what is the emergency? And what was it that these demonstrators were actually trying to accomplish on March 26th? Certainly a part of it was to eventually stop U.S. involvement in Central America, but what they demanded over and over and over again was, Senator Stafford, you call a meeting now to discuss these policies or we're not leaving. That was what they wanted.

Now, was that demand outweighed by criminal trespass? Is that such an emergency that he has to have this meeting right now when these wars have been going on and were going on that day, and are going on today? Was it such an emergency that they had no other choice of action but to break the law of the State of Vermont? And that, ladies and gentlemen, is the whole crux of what are we getting at here. Don't be drawn away from the initial reason why we are here, the unlawful trespass, by a smokescreen about what is going on in Central America. None of us can condone that. None of us would ever stand up and say that murder and atrocities are okay. Anyone who tries to say that Senator Stafford even thinks that, is being ridiculous. It simply is not the case.

However, my personal beliefs, the Defendants' beliefs, your personal beliefs, are not germane to the case which you have to decide. You have to look at the facts. You have to be objective, which you said you all could be when we drew the jury. And you have to put aside all personal prejudices and passions and say, bare bones in the cold light of a Vermont morning, what do we have here?

And what do we have? We have these twenty-six Defendants refusing to leave the United States Senator's office because they weren't getting what they wanted. The forty-four people arrested that morning refused to leave; and as a result the other five hundred thousand some odd people in Vermont did not have access to Senator Stafford's office that day if they wanted to.

I suggest, ladies and gentlemen, that when you deliberate over this question and you get into the juryroom, and for the first time you finally get a chance to sit down and start talking about this among yourselves, I am sure that you are going to have to say yes, the State has proven the elements of unlawful trespass beyond a reasonable doubt. And yes, testimony of the Defendants was compelling and maybe it's changed some of your minds. Maybe it's changed a lot of minds in this courtroom, but it's not of sufficient weight to allow them to invoke the necessity defense; for, if we do, where do we go from here? What then? What could be justified under the guise of necessity?

Ladies and gentlemen, it's been four long days. It's been very, very hot. As I told you when we began this trial, the jury system in the United States is maybe the toughest stone of our entire democracy and that's what you have to think about.

This is a democracy. You are jury members, and in a democracy, ladies and gentlemen, the majority rules. The minority may wail and gnash their teeth that they are not in power at the moment, but there are many other things that they can do to get in power.

I thank you all for your attention during the last four days. I appreciate the inconvenience that you have all gone through with your homes and your families, and I am confident that when you do get a chance to deliberate over this question, that you will return a verdict of guilty. Thank you very much.

For the Defense:

MS. BAUER: Ladies and gentlemen of the jury, thank you for your patience; thank you for your attention. This has been an extraordinary case and, yes, it is a hot courtroom; and that's probably about the only thing that Mr. Bradley and I agree on.

I think that the Defendants are very fortunate to be here today, to be tried by a jury of their peers who have been attentive throughout a very long trial, and who were sworn to judge them in accordance with the law that's going to be instructed by the Judge. And I think I hardly need to draw the comparison to some of the countries we have been discussing over the last few days, where that could not happen.

I think the issue is very much what is happening in Central America and I know that those of you who have been listening to the testimony over the last four days understand that my clients, when they were arrested in Senator Stafford's office on the 26th of March, were not involved in a simple trespass action; they were involved in an act of conscience. And that what they were doing was in a very real sense putting their bodies between the killing that's going on in Central America and the indifferent institutions of government that are allowing that to happen, in a very similar way to what the Witness for Peace participants described to you when they went down to El Salvador and to Nicaragua to put their bodies between the killers and the victims. These are serious matters, and it's our job here today to sum up for you a little bit about what you have heard over the last few days.

What I am going to do is first to talk briefly with you about the elements of the trespass statute. Next, I am going to talk briefly about a very important matter, the Defendants' right to freedom of speech. I will use that as a shorthand expression to freedom of speech under the United States Constitution and the Vermont Constitution, because there are a number of constitutional provisions that come to bear in this case. And then, finally, my colleague, Bill Dorsch, is going to talk to you about the necessity defense.

Here, Ms. Bauer gave several arguments related to the technicalities of the trespass statute.

The third element of trespass, which I think is very much in question here and is really a key element in this case, is that in order to find my clients guilty of trespass beyond a reasonable doubt, you must find that they were there without consent and without lawful authority. Consent and lawful authority — those are not the same thing.

Lawful authority does not have to be derived from a person in possession. There are higher sources of authority. The sources of authority that I want you to consider in this case, and the Judge will instruct you on this law, are the United States Constitution and the Vermont Constitution.

Now, the United States Constitution and the Vermont Constitution both say that citizens of this country, citizens of this state, have a right to freedom of speech. They have a right to freedom of petition. They have a right to assemble. And in the Vermont Constitution some of these rights are particularly stressed.

The Vermont Constitution says that people in this state have a right to assemble and instruct their elected officials. They have a right to hold their elected officials accountable to them at all times. Not just at election time; at all times. People in the State of Vermont have a right to alter and inform their government in any way that seems reasonable by their consciences. And it was in exercise of those rights that my clients were in Senator Stafford's office on the 26th of March, very much trying to breathe some life into these Constitutional provisions that make our democracy work.

And the State has complained to you. It has complained very much about all the trouble that was caused as a result of their actions and in a way that the office was unable to function.

How important is that? If you consider that as disruption and as disruptive activity, then I want you to consider what is happening in El Salvador, what is happening in Nicaragua, because I think that that lends some meaning to the word disruption. I think that thirty bombs a day being dropped on the civilian population, that is disruption.

And we heard testimony from Janet Shenk that those were American bombs; they were dropped by American planes that were led to their targets by American pilots. We heard Philippe Bourgois testify that he was caught in cross-fire for fourteen days. And that during that time the people that he was with, civilians and farmers, were rained with bullets. They were surveyed by helicopters. They escaped only because the world's attention was brought to that area for a moment by some television cameras.

Now those bullets, we found out again, are American bullets. They are made in this country, and they were fired from American guns. And there were American helicopters used in that action, and our taxpayers' dollars were used to perform those acts. And I submit to you that that is disruption. What was occurring in Senator Stafford's office was inconvenience.

I think, too, that the State would like to leave the impression with you that the only way these people have to communicate with their elected officials, is through demonstrations on the street, but please don't bother us too much, and please go home when it becomes inconvenient: Please, meet me behind closed doors; don't shed any public attention on these issues. But that's not what was vital to the Defendants.

The Defendants sought public debate on an issue of crucial and public importance. And I think that we have some very solid opinions on the citizens' rights to perceive that petitioning is not limited to letter writing.

One of our most memorable Supreme Court Justices, Justice William O. Douglas, has said, and I quote: "The right to petition for the redress of grievances has an ancient history, and it's not limited to writing a letter or sending a telegram to a congressman. It is not confined to appearing before the local city council or writing letters to the President or governor or mayor. Conventional methods of petitioning may be and often have been shut off to large groups of our citizens. Legislators may turn deaf ears; formal complaints may be routed endlessly through a bureaucratic maze; courts may let the wheels of justice grind very slowly. Those who do not control television and radio, those who cannot afford to produce newspapers or circulate elaborate pamphlets have only a more limited type of access to public officials. Their methods should not be condemned as tactics of obstruction and harassment as long as the assembly and petition are peaceable."

Now, all the evidence that you have heard in this case indicates to you that the Defendants' actions were peaceable, that the Defendants' actions were actions of conscience, and that the Defendants' actions were clearly within their right and their duty as citizens of a free society; and I submit to you that when you consider their actions in that light, you will acquit the Defendants of the crime of trespass. Thank you.

THE COURT: Thank you, Ms. Bauer. Mr. Dorsch?

MR. DORSCH: I am the last attorney for the Defendants who will speak to you in this case. I speak on behalf of all of us, and I speak with a great sense of pride for the extraordinary co-Counsel that I have had, and for the privilege of representing the twenty-six Defendants before you.

Now, throughout this trial you have sat over here and the Defendants have sat in the first three rows. Most of your interaction and most of what you have seen has been through witnesses on the stand and through Counsel on both sides. I would like to take a couple of minutes to re-introduce to you the Defendants so that you see who they are, who is before you today, charged with the crime of trespass: Sylvia Lane, Joanna Rankin, Paul Markowitz, Celia Oyler, Barr Swennerfelt, Abby Yasgur, Melrose Huff, Gil McCann, Joe Moore, Joy Hammond, John Rogers, Nancy Powell, David Dellinger, Robin Lloyd, Jeani Lowell, Jean Pineo, Eric Broque, Lea Terhune, Phil Fiermonte, Jennifer Strickler, and Jeanne Keller. Annie Gaillard, I believe she had to leave because her baby was not being as good as it's been the entire trial, but she is outside and she stands before you.

These people come from all walks of life. They come from all disciplines. They come from all ages and they place themselves in your hands as jurors.

Mr. Bradley has told you about the jury system and I agree with him. It is a great, great system. It isn't available to the people of El Salvador. It isn't available to many of the people of the world. It's available to the people of the United States. You sit in judgment of them and they trust you.

Now, as Joan told you, I am going to talk about the necessity defense. Mr. Bradley has talked some about the necessity defense and His Honor will charge you on the law of the necessity defense; but His Honor has indicated to us some of the things that he is going to tell you. And I will take the liberty to say one thing Mr. Bradley didn't tell you: that because the necessity defense has been raised and there has been evidence presented on it, His Honor will instruct you that the State must prove to you beyond a reasonable doubt that there wasn't a necessity, as opposed to our having to prove there was. They have to prove there wasn't.

Now, we believe there is no question the State has not proved to you that there wasn't a necessity, and I would point out to you for those of you who have been on criminal juries before, the standard is: beyond a reasonable doubt. His Honor will instruct you on what that means, and I know many of you are familiar with its terms.

Well, we feel that we have done much more than that. We're not asking you to find that there was a necessity because it isn't proved that there wasn't beyond a reasonable doubt. We're not asking you to say, well, we're going to find there was a necessity because the State hasn't proved it at all. We have come forward with affirmative evidence to show you that that necessity existed and that these people acted out of conscience, not only because of that necessity.

Now, Mr. Bradley has talked about elements of the necessity, and basically I agree with what he says the elements are; but I am going to talk a little bit differently just because it's easier for me to remember them this way.

The first one I'd like to talk about is whether or not there was an emergency in Central America. Well, we have put on a lot of evidence about that. The evidence has come from the witness stand, and it has ranged from the evidence of the Salvadoran refugees telling you about loved ones not only killed, but maimed; people for no reason picked up by death squads and killed, people tortured. Phillippe Bourgois talked about people hiding like animals in the woods for two weeks, chased by helicopters, chased by troops, shot at in a crossfire. In fact he, an anthropologist from Stanford University, was one of them. He fortunately got out. But the emergency continues, continues for people he left behind, the people who live there, the people who are hunted, the people who are subjected to the terror, the terror supported by the United States, by United States policy, the policy that witnesses told you violates international law, violates United States law; and I would submit that it violates moral law.

There is definitely an emergency in Central America. Now, Mr. Bradley talked some about whether or not that emergency would be solved by a demonstration or a meeting with Senator Stafford. And he said to you at one point that it's not his belief or my belief, or the Defendants' belief, as to what would be a reasonable way to deal with that emergency that counts. Well, His Honor, I believe, will instruct you that that's not true. It is relevant what the Defendants' beliefs are. It's very relevant. It's crucial, and you may consider it and you should consider it because their subjective belief about the emergency, and what is a reasonable way to meet that emergency, is absolutely essential to understand their actions and to realize the ultimate legality of what they did.

There are some other issues that came out through the witnesses' testimony, and I think one of the things they address is whether or not the harm or the criminal act of trespass outweighed the wrong these people were trying to overcome.

Now, I have thought about that. Sonia Hernandez' father, her fiancé, and some seventeen year old, were all killed. Is that fact more important and more severe than the fact that my clients may have trespassed in Senator Stafford's office? Is the fact that there was a trespass, if there was one by the Defendants, is that a more severe crime than the fact that these three people and thousands of other people in Central America are illegally being killed? Is the trespass more severe? It is not. It is not. The fact that people are being raped; the fact that international law is being broken; the fact that the United States is effecting illegal policies; is the trespass worse than any of those facts? I say it is not. The trespass is a minor act of civil disobedience in an attempt to stop the horrendous wrong going on in Central America. I really believe that it's irrefutable that the evidence has shown that the trespass itself was a minor act compared to the problems these people were trying to resolve in Central America.

Mr. Bradley has focused on the killing, saying, well, that's been going on for a long time, and it's not going to stop by a sit-in or by a meeting with Senator Stafford, or by his change of vote. And His Honor will instruct you that you may consider as an emergency, a continuing course of conduct: that killing after killing going on for years, and that may continue on for years, may be considered an emergency. It is a crucial issue that must be addressed and that these people were trying to address.

I think the ultimate issue is, have these people used a reasonable form of redress, a reasonable act to try and effect what they're trying to effect? His Honor will instruct you that it is not necessary that they accomplished anything by what they did. That is, they didn't have to show you that Senator Stafford's voting changed. Despite the State's numerous questions, they didn't have to show you that some lives were saved, some people didn't die in Central America, or that the United States stopped violating international law, or that the C.I.A. stopped lying to us, or that the United States stopped violating its own law. They didn't have to show that that was accomplished. The issue is whether or not what they did was a reasonable way to try and effect what they wanted, and whether or not there was any other course of action available to them.

Again, the State has attempted to elicit testimony from our clients about whether or not there were other methods of redress available. And I think that the Defendants have clearly shown that they have attempted some ways, met with some frustrations, and that in fact in the end their actions have been appreciated, and have had an effect. They have been appreciated by a Senator who has had an effect. They have been appreciated by a Senator who has changed his position. They wrote letters, they telephoned, they telegrammed, they attempted to meet. They petitioned, and petitioned, and petitioned, and it didn't work.

Now, when I say it didn't work, I don't mean it didn't change the vote. I mean it didn't get any response. Oh, it got a response, I guess. It got some form letters. It got an admission from the Senator saying, I'm not worried about Central America, that's not my field; a Senator whose vote is as important as other senators who do pay attention, who do learn, who do understand what is going on there. That was said by a Senator, who you heard, is a good Senator, a Senator who has been responsive in an area in which he is concerned, environmental issues; who has stood up in the Senate and opposed what he felt was a wrong policy of our administration.

So we have the Senator who is influential, who has listened, who is concerned, who now turns a deaf ear, a total deaf ear to a crucial emergency going on that our country is not only involved in, but creating and continuing.

The State would have you believe that the Defendants didn't do enough, that there were other things that they could have done. But these are peaceful people. These are people who aren't going to go and bomb places. The issue is, have they petitioned their government in a reasonable way? Have they met with a stone wall? Yes, yes; they have repeatedly. So they took the action they took, and I believe the evidence clearly shows that in the end it was the best action because it got results.

Now, I'd like to go back again and say, please keep in mind that when His Honor instructs you, he is going to say we don't have to show you that there was a necessity. They have to show you beyond a reasonable doubt that there wasn't. So we don't have to show you that there is an emergency, but we have. The emergency is the killing, all of the horrendous details you heard about Central America. And the emergency is the influence and importance of the issues that involve Central America. And as you heard from the witnesses today, a senator is influenced by constituents and responds to demonstrations, responds to petitions, responds to strong advocacy by his constituents.

We don't have to show you that the emergency was perceived by the Defendants. The State has to show you that it wasn't perceived, but we have shown you that it was perceived. We didn't have to show you that the emergency outweighed the wrong committed by the Defendants. The State has to show you beyond a reasonable doubt that that was not the case. We have shown it was. And we didn't have to show you that the Defendants' actions were reasonable and that they had no other course of action that eliminated other reasonable courses of action. We didn't have to show that; again, the State has to show you beyond a reasonable doubt, but we showed you. It took a few days, it took a lot of witnesses, but we showed you that.

When I knew that I was speaking to you today, I tried to figure out what I was going to say. And one of the things that occurred to me was that I voted a week ago, and I assumed that most or all of you did, also. And as I voted, as I have for about twenty years, for the first time I felt very different in the voting booth. As I walked into the voting place I passed by a man holding a placard for one of the gubernatorial candidates; and I'll tell you, if you don't tell anybody, but that wasn't the candidate I was going to vote for. And I walked in and I voted, and then I came out, and as I came out, trying to be very friendly, I said hello to him. At that time we were preparing this trial, and we were talking a lot about how we would present the evidence to you people. And I was hearing a lot from attorneys who had talked to various witnesses about what would be presented by the expert witnesses. And I realized that I was able to go and vote, and I had no concerns whatsoever for my safety. I knew I could walk by this person holding the placard and, you know, he wasn't going to ask me who I voted for. He wasn't going to punish me in some way. My children worked for one of the gubernatorial candidates. And unlike the seventeen-year-old in El Salvador, unlike what happened to that young man, I have no concern about their safety. They can speak publicly about who they felt should win and they did. They can be seen doing it and it's safe regardless of whether the candidate wins or loses. That's not available in Central America, and you heard how unavailable it is.

You also heard about the kind of protest that is not only accepted and respected in this country, but respected worldwide; protests ranging from the Boston Tea Party to actions taken to abolish slavery, and through into this century. And strong protests that greatly influenced our government about a policy in southeast Asia that was ultimately found to be against our best interests. These people who are before you today and who ask for your consideration, are a part of that tradition.

As I was sitting around last night I picked up the *New York Times* and there was an article about a person who is very famous to all the lawyers here. I think his name is Clarence Gideon. I guess he was a bum in Florida in 1960, and he had a very, very long record. It was all really nothing that serious, but just crime after crime. He went before a court in Florida and he was tried without an attorney. He was locked up and then he started petitioning various courts. Ultimately, he petitioned the United States Supreme Court, and he asked that the Supreme Court appoint a lawyer for him. He said, this isn't fair; I didn't have a lawyer at this trial. The Supreme Court asked a Washington attorney by the name of Abe Fortes to represent him. And Clarence Gideon and Abe Fortes together created an incredibly important law; that everybody has a right to an attorney, and if they can't afford an attorney in a criminal matter, the Court will appoint an attorney.

As I was reading this article I came to the end and I read this one part where Gideon wrote to Fortes, right before the argument before the United States Supreme Court; and what he said was: "I believe that each error finds improvement in law; maybe this will be one of those small steps forward."

Well, my clients believe that every error finds improvement in communications between constituents and congresspeople, improvement in the United States policy, improvement in the world.

They are not telling you that what they did changed the world. They're telling you that what they did was one step, and that was a step forward; and they are confident that when you deliberate you will agree that what they did, did not break the law of the State of Vermont. Thank you.

THE COURT: Thank you, Mr. Dorsch. Mr. Bradley?

MR. BRADLEY: Thank you, Your Honor. Very briefly, ladies and gentlemen, I would just like to go over a few things the Defense touched upon in their closing argument. Ms. Bauer said that the people of the United States are guaranteed by the United States Constitution and the Vermont Constitution, that they have a right to petition their government and to change their government in any reasonable way. And you heard them say that we have a right as American citizens to petition our elected officials. We do have that right. We have always had that right, but the elected officials also have a right, ladies and gentlemen. And that is to listen to what people are saying and, for one reason or another, to disregard what they are saying.

There is no right to have your elected official take everything that is said to him or her to heart and vote on that. They have to look at the greater issue. They have to look at what the majority wants, and simply because a few people are complaining, does not mean that everything has to stop and that he has to go or address that particular issue. I suggest to you, if that were to be the case, that our system of Congress would fall apart completely.

With the necessity defense, it is the burden of the State, as the Judge will explain to you, to prove beyond a reasonable doubt that there was no necessity, and I think we have met that burden. We have told you about the four elements of the defense. The third and most crucial element in the State's perspective, is that there can be no reasonable alternative open to the people who are taking the action.

There were plenty of reasonable alternatives. All they had to do was move ten feet from inside the office door to the outside, and continue their protest. And that was a reasonable alternative. If that were the only one, there would still be a failure of that crucial element in the necessity defense, but it wasn't. There were plenty of other things that could be done.

The Defendants themselves testified that throughout the previous week there had been many different things staged and planned not only in Vermont, but throughout the entire United States, dealing with Central America. There were many different alternatives, all of them reasonable, that the Defendants could have taken.

And the last thing I'd like to leave with you, is to remind you what it was that these people were asking for on March 26th. They were asking for a public meeting. That was their emergency. That's what they were asking for. And I submit to you that the request for a public meeting does not outweigh the offense of criminal trespass.

In this country, ladies and gentlemen, as a democracy, you are allowed to petition your government. You are allowed to try and change the views of your senators. You are allowed to oust them from office by electing someone else. The place to determine the policy of the United States and who is going to be representing you, ladies and gentlemen, is in the ballot box. It's in the rooms where we vote, and where we have voted for two hundred years. It's not in the courtroom, ladies and gentlemen. This is a criminal courtroom, and it is not the place to determine the foreign policy of the United States. Thank you.

THE COURT: Thank you, Mr. Bradley.

Court's Charge to the Jury

THE COURT: First of all, I would very much like to thank all of the lawyers involved: Mr. Bradley, Ms. Shingler, Mr. Dorsch, Mr. McGill, Ms. Baird, Ms. Vance, Ms. Bauer, Mr. McCullough, Mr. Nelson, and Ms. Black. It's been, I am sure, a difficult case to prepare and present, and all of the attorneys involved have done so very, very well, in my opinion; and I think the case has been extremely well tried by all Counsel, and at least as important, if not more important, very professionally tried. And I very, very much appreciate it. It makes me proud to be a lawyer, and I thank you folks very much.

Also, with the number of people we have had in the courtroom throughout the course of the past four days, there's bound to be some disruption and some distraction, and I realize it's been fairly uncomfortable in here as well, particularly the temperature level; and I very much appreciate the cooperation of all you folks in keeping that to a minimum given how many people were here, and I do appreciate it.

I am going to appoint Mrs. Bedard as the foreperson of this jury. It will be Mrs. Bedard's responsibility to preside over your deliberations and to announce your verdicts.

As you folks know from your previous experience, now that you have heard the evidence in the case and the arguments of the Counsel, it becomes my job to visit with you for a while about the legal principles that apply to this particular case, and it then becomes your job to take those legal principles and apply them to the facts in the case as you find the facts to exist. You folks are the sole judges of the facts and you take the law as given by the Court.

You should understand that you shouldn't attempt to single out any one legal principle alone as stating the law, but rather try to consider the legal principles involved as a whole. Very obviously it would be improper of me to frame my comments on what the legal principles in the case are, based on any personal opinion that I might have as to what the law should be. That would be a very serious breach of my oath of office.

We frame the comments on the applicable law from the materials available from our Constitutions, statutes, and case law, and most certainly not on any judge's personal opinion of what the law should be. By the same token, of course you are obligated to take the law as stated here in court, and not substitute your personal opinions as to what you might think the law should or should not be. That would be a very serious breach of your oath as jurors.

You also are aware that you shouldn't let your empathies, either for or against any of the parties in this case, influence your fair and just determination of the facts in the case, or your reporting of a verdict under the applicable law as stated here in court.

You of course may not, under our system of justice, pass a verdict of guilty on mere conjecture or speculation, but only upon proof beyond a reasonable doubt. The fact that these Defendants are here under information and on trial, is not to be taken against them in any way whatsoever. As I have indicated to you previously, the information filed by the State's Attorney's office is simply a piece of paper with a charge on it, and absolutely nothing more. It is no evidence whatsoever of any of the Defendants' guilt. It's simply an accusation which starts the criminal process underway, which charges the Defendants with the particular offense; and you should not be influenced in the slightest degree by the fact that the information was filed, or that these folks are here on trial. Their guilt can only be established by the evidence presented here in court. The credibility, I prefer believability, of witnesses, and the weight which you will give to the testimony of the witnesses, are questions which are entirely for your determination.

The law is that you are not bound to give the same weight to the testimony of each witness, but you should give the testimony of each witness just that weight which you think it's properly entitled to receive. It is perfectly proper for you to believe all of a particular witness's testimony. It is also perfectly proper for you to disbelieve the entirety of a particular witness' testimony. By the same token, it's perfectly proper for you to believe part of a given witness' testimony while disbelieving other parts of that same witness' testimony.

There are many things that you may consider in determining the believability of witnesses, and the proper weight to be given to their testimony. I am going to list just a few of the things which it is proper for you to consider in going about that task, but I don't mean this list of things to be in any way exclusive. It's just by way of examples of the types of things you may consider when determining believability and weight to be given to the evidence.

It's perfectly proper for you to consider the demeanor of a witness on the witness stand; how did the witness appear to you? How did he or she act? It is proper for you to consider the candor or lack of candor of the witness. Is the witness being straightforward with you? The feeling or bias, if any, of a witness, or a witness' interest in how the trial comes out, are perfectly proper for your consideration.

You may also consider the opportunity for observation, the means of information that the witness had as to the matter that he or she testified about. How did the witness come to know the matters about which the witness is giving testimony? Finally, you may consider the inherent reasonableness of the testimony itself. Does it make sense? That's a perfectly proper consideration.

In short, the credibility of the witnesses, the believability if you will, of the witnesses, and the weight to be attached to their testimony, are entirely matters for your sound, practical judgment as fair-minded men and women.

Some of the testimony which has been introduced in this case has been what we call expert testimony. Expert testimony is to be weighed by you along with all the other evidence in the case. An expert is a person who, by reason of special study, training and experiences as to a given subject such as history or political science, has knowledge concerning that subject which is superior to the rest of us in general. Such a witness is often allowed to testify as to his opinion on the subject matter involved in his area of expertise, whereas other witnesses are not allowed to express such opinions.

The value of expert testimony, or the opinions given by an expert, depends upon the honesty and ability of the witness, and upon the facts used by the witness as a basis for his opinion. If the facts used by the witness as a basis for his opinion are proved by other evidence in the case, and his qualifications are high, and he is honest and impartial, his opinion may be of great value to you in deciding the issues in this case.

On the other hand, if the witness' opinion is based upon a fact which the rest of the evidence in the case doesn't sustain, or if the witness is incompetent or dishonest, or not impartial, his testimony may be of little or no value to you in deciding the issues in the case. The weight to be given expert testimony and the opinions of expert witnesses is just like any other evidence in the case, and the weight to be placed upon it is solely a matter for your determination.

In this case the Defendants have been charged by an information which alleges that at Winooski, in the County of Chittenden, on the 26th day of March, 1984, they were then and there people who without legal authority or the consent of the persons in lawful possession, Raymond Pecor and Rey Post, remained in Senator Robert Stafford's office, located in the Champlain Mill, as to which notice against trespass had been given by actual communication by the person in lawful possession, Raymond Pecor and Rey Post, and by a law enforcement officer, Barry Lawrence, acting on behalf of Raymond Pecor and Rey Post.

It's an allegation of unlawful trespass. It is helpful to analyze the offense charged by breaking it down into what lawyers call essential elements, and to look at each of the important parts of the particular offense charged, separately.

With regard to the offense of unlawful trespass, there are three separate and distinct essential elements. It is the burden of the State to establish all three of those essential elements beyond a reasonable doubt. If the State establishes only two of them beyond a reasonable doubt, then your verdict must be not guilty. Analytically, this offense breaks down in these three parts.

First, that the Defendants entered or remained in any place. That's the first element.

Second, that notice against trespass was given by actual communication by the person in lawful possession, or his agent, or a law enforcement office acting on behalf of such a person.

And third, that the Defendant was there without legal authority, or the consent of the person in lawful possession. In this regard, the First Amendment to the United States Constitution guarantees to all citizens the right of freedom of speech, freedom of assembly, and freedom to petition government representatives.

In addition to the First Amendment to the United States Constitution, there are also applicable provisions of our own Vermont Constitution; and the

Vermont Constitution is a document of equal dignity and equal importance with the United States Constitution. Indeed, it predates the United States Constitution.

Our own State Constitution provides, among other things, that all power being originally inherent and consequently derived from the people, therefore, all officers of government, whether legislative or executive, are their trustees and servants, and at all times, in a legal way, accountable to them. Our own State Constitution also provides that government is, or ought to be, instituted for the common benefit, protection and security of the people, nation or community, and not for the particular emolument or advantage of any single man, family, or set of men who are only a part of that community. And that the community has the indubitable, unalienable, indefeasible right to reform or alter government in such manner as shall be, by that community, judged most conducive to the public weal. So, in considering whether the Defendants were there without legal authority, it is proper for you to consider those Constitutional provisions of both our Federal and State Constitutions.

Of course those rights are not absolute and unlimited rights. As Mr. Justice Holmes once observed, the First Amendment does not protect the right to yell "fire, fire" in a crowded movie theater. Such rights may be limited, but they are fundamental rights, and they are Constitutional rights and, therefore, rights of the highest order.

Citizens, therefore, have a right to petition their government for redress of grievances. They have a right to peaceful and orderly expression of their views in settings traditional for civic debate. They have a right to assemble together to instruct their elected representatives. They have a right to request that their elected representatives be accountable to them. If you find that the Defendants were engaged in the exercise of these rights, and they were arrested because of their activities, you may not find them guilty of unlawful trespass unless the State also proves beyond a reasonable doubt that the State's actions in restricting their exercise of these rights, served a significant State interest and, further, that their regulation of these important rights were reasonable as to time, place and manner.

The defense of necessity is well recognized in the law and was explicitly recognized as being the law in the State of Vermont by our own State Supreme Court within the past year. It is a defense with a long history. However, it is a doctrine which is one of specific application, as a defense to criminal behavior. This is so because, if the qualifications for the defense of necessity are not closely delineated, the definition of criminal activity may become uncertain and even whimsical. So it is important in applying the defense that has been presented, the defense of necessity, that you do it in terms of four well-established, analytical elements of that defense which have been laid down by our State Supreme Court. In other words, it is not a political referendum or an election. It is a legal principle and must be analyzed by you in terms of the legal criteria set forth by our Supreme Court for analyzing that defense. Essentially, the defense of necessity will apply if the four elements apply to the factual situation. And with regard to these elements, it is also the burden of the State to prove beyond a reasonable doubt, necessity did not exist or apply.

The four elements which must prevail are as follows: first, there must be a situation of emergency arising without fault on the part of the actor involved; in other words, without fault of the Defendants.

Secondly, this emergency must be so imminent and compelling as to raise a reasonable expectation of harm, either directly to the Defendant or upon those he was seeking to protect.

Thirdly, the emergency must present no reasonable opportunity to avoid the injury without committing the unlawful act; in this case, the alleged unlawful trespass.

Fourth, the injury impending from the emergency must be of sufficient seriousness to outweigh the criminal wrong that has been alleged, the criminal wrong of unlawful trespass.

The first element is a situation of emergency arising without fault on the part of the Defendant. I think that's pretty much self-explanatory.

Secondly, this emergency must be so imminent and compelling as to raise a reasonable expectation of harm upon those the Defendant was seeking to protect. In this regard I'd like to look at both the concept of imminent, and the concept of harm. The emergency must reasonably appear to the Defendant to be threatening to occur immediately, near at hand in terms of time, though not necessarily geographically. The harm need not be unique or one of a kind, or a one-shot type of harm. However, it must be a harm which is reasonably certain to occur. It's not a harm which is merely speculative or uncertain.

Third, this emergency must present no reasonable opportunity to avoid the injury without committing the unlawful trespass. And the question that you have to ask there is, was it reasonably conceived by the Defendant to have been a necessity? In other words, the test is one of reasonable subjectivity. Did the Defendant in fact conceive that his or her actions were a necessity, and was the Defendant reasonable in so conceiving the situation?

Fourth, the injury impending from the emergency must be of sufficient seriousness to outweigh the criminal wrong, or the unlawful trespass. And this element involves a weighing of values. Did the emergency which the Defendants claim they were responding to, was that of sufficient seriousness to outweigh the alleged criminal trespass? And here again, the test is one of reasonable subjectivity, and the relevant question is, did the Defendant reasonably believe that the need, as the Defendant conceived that need to be, outweighed the criminal wrong?

It is also necessary to ask, did the Defendant reasonably believe that his or her action would avoid the harm? And in this regard, it is not important whether the Defendant was ultimately successful or not in meeting the emergency situation.

In this situation of determining whether or not the impending injury from the emergency situation was of sufficient weight to outweigh the alleged unlawful trespass, you should understand that the threatened harm that was perceived by the Defendant need not have been a criminal act, or a crime. An emergency situation of that type could be, as one of the attorneys described, a fire in a house. On the other hand, you may, if you choose, consider whether or not the government of the United States was violating international law with regard to the alleged emergency situation which the Defendants indicated that they perceived. That is appropriate for you to consider in weighing the values involved under this fourth element.

You should understand that international law is law. It is law which is binding on the United States of America and on the State of Vermont, and so it is appropriate for your consideration. Some of the principles of international law which are relevant for your consideration in this regard include the Resolutions of the United Nations which were supported by the United States of America, as well as provisions of the Charter of the Organization of American States of which the United States of America is a signatory. Under those it is a principle of international law binding on the United States of America and the State of Vermont, and no state or group of states has the right to intervene directly, or indirectly, for any reason whatsoever, in the internal or external affairs of any other state or nation. This principle applies not only to armed forces, but to any other form of interference, or attempted interference. International law specifically prohibits the organization or the encouragement of the organization of armed bands for incursion into the territory of another state or another nation, the undertaking or encouragement of activities calculated to foment civil strife in another nation, or the undertaking or encouragement of terroristic activities in another nation.

Also under the Geneva Protocols, which are binding on the United States of America, it is a violation of international law for one country to associate in the crimes of another state. And under the Geneva Protocols, any indiscriminate act of terror aimed at civilians is a violation of international law, and such an act of terror includes violence to life and person, murder of all kinds, mutilation, cruel treatment, and torture.

The taking of hostages, outrages upon personal dignity, and humiliating or degrading treatment, are violations of international law. Acts of terrorism and collective punishments against civilian populations are likewise violations of international law. And it is appropriate for you to consider those legal principles in weighing the relative value of the injuries which the Defendants claim they saw impending from the perceived emergency in Central America against the seriousness of the criminal trespass allegedly committed by them.

The Defendants, each of them, are presumed to be innocent of the charges. This very important principle of our judicial system is narrowly-enough called the presumption of innocence. What it means is that although accused, the Defendant is innocent at the beginning of the trial; and this presumption of innocence stays with the Defendant throughout the trial and throughout your deliberations, right down to the very moment when you folks reach a verdict.

The presumption itself is a piece of evidence which you should consider in the Defendants' favor in deciding whether that Defendant is guilty or innocent. You should discuss this presumption during the course of your deliberations, as it is an important consideration for you during your deliberations. The presumption of innocence means that you must find a Defendant not guilty unless after careful and impartial consideration of all the evidence in the case, you are satisfied beyond a reasonable doubt that the Defendant is indeed guilty.

This presumption of innocence alone is sufficient to acquit a Defendant unless you are satisfied beyond a reasonable doubt of his guilt from all the evidence in the case. It's up to the State to prove, beyond a reasonable doubt, that the Defendant is guilty. This burden remains on the State throughout the trial, and it never, ever shifts to a Defendant. A Defendant, under our system of justice, does not have to prove that he or she is innocent. The burden throughout is on the State to prove that he or she is guilty beyond a reasonable doubt.

Of course the State does not have to prove a Defendant guilty beyond all possible doubt. The test is one of reasonable doubt. A reasonable doubt is a real doubt which is based on reason and common sense, which comes from a fair and rational consideration of the evidence or the lack of evidence in the case. It's not a vague, speculative or imaginary doubt. Proof beyond a reasonable doubt must be proof which is so convincing that reasonable folks such as yourselves would not hesitate to act upon it in matters of your own personal lives, or in the lives of your family. Proof beyond a reasonable doubt is proof to a moral certainty.

A Defendant is not to be convicted on mere suspicion or conjecture, or merely if you find it is more likely that he or she is guilty than not. Suspicion alone, no matter how strong, does not constitute proof beyond a reasonable doubt.

Any evidence which has been excluded or stricken from the record is not evidence in the case and should not be considered by you folks during your deliberations. The State's comments and comments of the defense lawyers, while helpful to you in understanding the case and understanding their theories of the case, is not evidence and should not be considered by you as evidence in your deliberations. The only evidence is the sworn testimony from the witness stand, and any exhibits that may have been admitted into testimony. Your verdict must represent the considered judgment of every one of you. In order to return a verdict it is necessary that each of you agree to that verdict. Your verdict must be unanimous. In this particular case there will be twenty-six separate verdicts. You must reach a verdict of guilty or not guilty as to each and every one of the twenty-six separate Defendants. When you are brought back here to court, I will ask Mrs. Bedard as to your verdict as to each and every individual Defendant by name.

Your verdict, of course, will be oral. When you have arrived at a verdict you should make this fact known to the court officer, but you should not tell the court officer what that verdict is. You folks will then be brought into the courtroom. Mrs. Bedard will be asked if you have reached your verdict, and if she answers in the affirmative I will then ask what your verdict is as to each of the individual Defendants, specifically by name; and Mrs. Bedard will reply guilty or not guilty as your verdict may be.

The Delivery of the Verdict

Jury returns to the courtroom.

THE COURT: Mrs. Bedard, has the jury reached a verdict, ma'am?

MRS. BEDARD: Yes.

THE COURT: Very well. If the Defendants would please stand and face the jury? The jury would please stand and face the Defendants.

Mrs. Bedard, as to the Defendant Jeanne Keller, how does the jury find — guilty or not guilty?

MRS. BEDARD: Not guilty.

THE COURT: Please, please. As to the Defendant Joy Hammond, how does the jury find the Defendant — guilty or not guilty?

MRS. BEDARD: Not guilty.

THE COURT: As to the Defendant, Melrose Huff?

MRS. BEDARD: Not guilty.

THE COURT: As to the Defendant, Sylvia Lane?

MRS. BEDARD: Not guilty.

THE COURT: As to the Defendant, Joseph Moore?

MRS. BEDARD: Not guilty.

THE COURT: As to the Defendant, David Dellinger?

MRS. BEDARD: Not guilty.

THE COURT: As to the Defendant, Phil Fiermonte?

MRS. BEDARD: Not guilty.

THE COURT: As to the Defendant, Annie Gaillard?

MRS. BEDARD: Not guilty.

THE COURT: As to the Defendant, Robin Lloyd?

MRS. BEDARD: Not guilty.

THE COURT: As to the Defendant, Gil McCann?

MRS. BEDARD: Not guilty.

THE COURT: As to the Defendant, Paul Markowitz?

MRS. BEDARD: Not guilty.

THE COURT: As to the Defendant, Celia Oyler?

MRS. BEDARD: Not guilty.

THE COURT: As to the Defendant, Nancy Powell?
MRS. BEDARD: Not guilty.
THE COURT: As to the Defendant, John Rogers?
MRS. BEDARD: Not guilty.
THE COURT: As to the Defendant, Gary Sisco?
MRS. BEDARD: Not guilty.
THE COURT: As to the Defendant, Jennifer Strickler?
MRS. BEDARD: Not guilty.
THE COURT: As to the Defendant, Barr Swennerfelt?
MRS. BEDARD: Not guilty.
THE COURT: As to the Defendant, Leonara Terhune?
MRS. BEDARD: Not guilty.
THE COURT: As to the Defendant, John Van Raalte, Junior?
MRS. BEDARD: Not guilty.
THE COURT: As to the Defendant, Nicholas Velvet?
MRS. BEDARD: Not guilty.
THE COURT: As to the Defendant, Abby Yasgur?
MRS. BEDARD: Not guilty.
THE COURT: As to the Defendant, Joanna Rankin?
MRS. BEDARD: Not guilty.
THE COURT: As to the Defendant, Jean Pineo?
MRS. BEDARD: Not guilty.
THE COURT: As to the Defendant, Rose Reilly?
MRS. BEDARD: Not guilty.
THE COURT: As to the Defendant, Jeani Lowell?
MRS. BEDARD: Not guilty.
THE COURT: As to the Defendant, Eric Brocque?
MRS. BEDARD: Not guilty.
THE COURT: Very well. And so say you all, ladies and gentlemen?
THE JURY: Yes.

Appendix

Conference: Testimony by Richard Falk Regarding International Law

This conference took place in the judge's chambers after the presentation of evidence and before the closing arguments.

Witness Richard Falk resumed the stand.

THE COURT: I thought, Professor Falk, that you might be able to help me with any relevant provisions of the Charter of the Organization of American States, the Geneva Protocols, and any treaty provisions that are relative to American blockades or embargoes.

MR. FALK: Well, I don't have all of those legal texts here with me. The Charter is an international treaty that has been fully ratified by the United States, and, therefore, is entitled to be treated as supreme law of the land.

The most fundamental ideas contained in the Charter in Article 24 involve an unconditional renunciation of the right to use force as an instrument of foreign policy. That's qualified by Article 51, to the extent that force can be used in self-defense provided it is reported immediately to the Security Council to see whether it was an appropriate use of self-defense.

Article 33 notes that there is an obligation to resolve international disputes by peaceful means. I think the Charter is sort of a fundamental organic law of international relations that rests on these two ideas: that force cannot be used except in self-defense, and that peaceful settlement is the first obligation of a state when it finds itself in a dispute with another country.

The Charter prohibits intervention in the internal affairs of a sovereign state. It is very consistently emphasized in the western hemisphere and has meant a great deal to the Latin American governments that have pressed the United States to accept this notion over the years.

Prohibition of intervention is also reinforced by General Assembly resolutions that the United States has supported and can be viewed as binding on the United States, even if the resolution itself isn't binding because it's a recommendation of the Assembly. Those states that support the resolution are viewed according to most international law commentaries as having accepted those principles.

The laws of war aspect of international law that are present here are quite complex. The most pertinent international instrument is probably the second Geneva Protocol of 1977, which tries to place internal wars and international wars within a framework of international law, and is viewed generally as international law even for governments that have not ratified that convention. And the two broad ideas that are implicit in the Geneva Protocol are, first of all, that conflict be conducted in such a way as to spare innocent civilians. The indirect or direct perpetration of acts of war, directed at civilians, is a violation of international law even in an undeclared war.

And secondly, the tactics and methods of warfare have to have some regard for the military character of the objective; they have to be proportional, discriminating, and in general not acts of terror aimed indiscriminately at the society.

There is, in addition, the very closely related idea that it is a violation of international law to foment civil strife in a foreign country. That's contained in the declaration of general principles of international law concerning friendly relations, it's present in our own domestic neutrality act, and it's present in the 1907 Hague convention regarding the right and duties of neutral powers and persons in case of war on land. And it's been very strongly reinforced by the United Nations General Assembly resolutions which, I believe, have been unanimous. It's also contained in the non-intervention conventions. Therefore, any activity in terms of recruiting, training, guiding, or providing mercenaries for harassing the governing process of a legitimate government with which we're at peace would represent a clear violation of these various legal authorities. That would apply to Nicaragua. Any activities of that sort that are intended to destabilize or foment violence in Nicaragua would be such a violation. Similarly, any association with an on-going civil strife of the sort that exists in Central America that associated the United States with crimes of state in El Salvador would be viewed as a violation of international law. And both of these kinds of indirect participation in illegal acts were confirmed at the Nuremberg Trials at the end of World War II. The Nuremberg Trials also lead to individual responsibility for the leader of the responsible government. In other words, the idea was extended there that those who performed violations of international law, or who are responsible for the policies that produce those violations, are individually accountable, and that there is some obligation on the part of the citizens to enforce that accountability on their own government.

President Roosevelt, during World War II, sent a very famous message to the German people in which he urged them to gather evidence of the criminality of their leaders' policies and to do whatever they could to obstruct that criminality because a higher law was more relevant than the law of the state. And I think that the United States, particularly, has stood for the proposition that there is really a higher law at issue than that which is determined by the national government in the event the two are in conflict with one another. By virtue of the supremacy clause, international agreements are the supreme law of the land unless there is a directly contrary Congressional enactment at a later date that would then take precedence.

Would you like me to elaborate on any of these?

THE COURT: No, that's very helpful. One other area I was curious about was the legality of economic blockades and embargoes.

MR. FALK: Well, I cannot give you very precise citations, but part of the concept of nonintervention is a prohibition on using economic coercion in order to alter the policy of another government. It is viewed as a species of intervention, particularly when it is deliberately designed to interfere with the normal exercise of sovereign rights of the other country. And, again, the United Nations has quite frequently declared that economic coercion is inconsistent with upholding international law and upholding the United Nations Charter. Establishing a blockade is really beyond that prohibition and is generally regarded in international law as an act of war, if it is attempting to interfere with the fundamental right of a state to participate in the international economy.

THE COURT: That was one of the reasons we cited in getting into the First World War, wasn't it?

MR. FALK: Yes. And it was also relevant in the more recent OPEC embargo. We claimed that we had the right, that we didn't exercise, that if this was producing any kind of economically adverse effect on vital interests, there would be a retaliatory intervention. And of course it was one of the explanations that the Japanese give for recourse to war against us in 1941. In the dissenting opinions of the Tokyo war crimes trials, the Indian judge regarded the economic aggression against Japan as making it impossible to really draw the legal conclusion that they had engaged in aggression, that there is a kind of self-defense for economic interests as well as for physical interests in response to military attack.

THE COURT: Thank you very much, sir.

Appendix

Charge Conference: Discussion of the Necessity Defense

This conference in the judge's chambers preceded the presentation of closing arguments.

THE COURT: Very well. I guess the first issue to be addressed is whether or not the necessity defense should be submitted to the jury. Do you wish to address that, Ms. Shingler?

MS. SHINGLER: Yes, Your Honor. It's my understanding that state of law in Vermont as it stands now, that before the issue of a necessity defense is presented to the jury, the Defendants have to present at least some evidence as to all of the four elements. Although it is clear that they have presented some evidence on some of the elements, there is one element of the necessity defense upon which there has been no evidence submitted: the element as to reasonable alternatives. I believe that the evidence presented by the Defendants clearly demonstrates that there were alternative methods to avert the tragedy in Central America; they have brought on experts, one after the other, that have indicated that, although sitting-in is a traditional form of civil disobedience, it is one form among many. I believe that the necessity defense requires that there is no reasonable alternative.

THE COURT: It's a subjective test, though, is it not? It's no reasonable alternative in the reasonable perception of the Defendants.

MS. SHINGLER: This is true. And I believe that they have not presented such evidence. I believe certain of the Defendants have also taken the stand and indicated that there were other methodologies which they could have used and that they were contemplating. Their expert witnesses have also demonstrated that there are reasonable alternatives. It appears that they have relied on the tradition of civil disobedience in our country, and reliance on that tradition would indicate to all of the Defendants that they did not have one source of recourse left, that there were alternatives, and the Defendants, those that have taken the stand, have actually admitted that they participated in reasonable alternatives and they they actually knew that there were reasonable alternatives; that they chose to take that one because they were frustrated by Senator Stafford's position and his unwillingness to meet their demands.

THE COURT: Doesn't Mr. Justice Peck in *State v. Shotton*, however, tell us that the question of reasonableness is for the jury, not for me?

MS. SHINGLER: I believe that the reasonableness question is for the jury and not for you, but I believe that the *Shotton* Court also says that there has to be some evidence that there was no reasonable alternative before it goes to the jury. I believe that's clear in *Shotton*, and I believe it's clear here that that element has not been satisfied. And, therefore, I would ask that the Court not instruct the jury on the defense of necessity based on the fact that they have not shown some evidence that there was no reasonable alternative.

THE COURT: Very well. Ms. Shingler, do you have something further on that?

MS. SHINGLER: Yes. I just wanted to point out that they had a series of alternatives on March 26th, 1984, that were presented to them. Mr. Pecor had indicated to them they could stay in the hallway for two weeks, rent free, and then after that maybe have to work out an arrangement. They had this alternative that was reasonable to everybody that was there.

There was also another reasonable alternative and that was Senator Stafford's willingness that certain representatives could meet with him. It was not exactly what they wanted, but it was a reasonable alternative. Therefore, I would ask that the Court not instruct. I think it's clear that there were many reasonable alternatives, and it's been clear through the last three days.

THE COURT: Thank you, Ms. Shingler. Mr. Nelson?

MR. NELSON: Your Honor, I would submit that the Defendants have submitted compelling evidence on each of the elements of the necessity defense. I would agree with the State's characterization of our burden to put forth some evidence on each of those elements.

I won't argue the evidence that we think we have established on the other elements of the defense, turning only to this question of whether there were alternative methods. Certainly the Defendants have put on some evidence, to understate, the matter on the absence of reasonable alternatives. The Defendants themselves have evidence that they reasonably felt that things had reached the point with Senator Stafford, and his refusals to meet with them, that nothing was left to them except this action, morally and practically.

Sitting-in in the hallway might be a method of influencing Mr. Pecor in some respect. Mr. Pecor's opinion about Central America would have no effect, of course. It was Senator Stafford that they were trying to influence. The offer that was made to them fell short, yes, of what they felt was the only thing that would do any good: namely, a public and open meeting on the subject.

I don't think it's necessary to go specifically over the evidence of each of the Defendants, but I think that we can all recall that a number of them said they felt they had no alternatives. I would submit that this is proof of a sincere belief of an absence of alternatives, that the other evidence that we have established through Mr. Zinn this morning, and through other witnesses, indicated that that belief, that sincere belief was also a reasonable one.

THE COURT: I would like Mr. Nelson if he would, to address, generally, how I should analytically approach the necessity defense in view of former Chief Justice Barney's comment in *State v. Warshow*, in terms of how stringent and narrowing the defense should be defined. Chief Justice Barney indicated "the doctrine is one of specific application insofar as it's a defense to criminal behavior. This is clear because the qualifications for the defense of necessity are not closely delineated." That's really the phrase I had in mind.

The definition of "criminal activity" becomes uncertain and even whimsical. And I noted Chief Justice Barney's warning even more when I went back and reread *Warshow* after doing some research more generally on the necessity defense, and I think my concern and Chief Justice Barney's concern is that the necessity defense has not historically been used in situations like this, but has been used as an escape mechanism, if you will, for arbitrary and high-handed unconstitutional behavior by the State. I am thinking of *United States v. Matthew*, probably one of the worst decisions of our United States Supreme Court, where the necessity defense was used by the government to justify arbitrary action.

I am thinking of the case of Bisby Deportations where law enforcement officers justified kidnapping people, or the similar situation in the Dorr's Rebellion case in Massachusetts; and isn't it a very dangerous defense and a real two-edged sword, and shouldn't I follow Chief Justice Barney's caution very carefully?

MR. NELSON: I think it's a real concern and I think that the whimsical application of the necessity defense is a danger. I'm not sure exactly what Chief Justice Barney meant by closely defining the terms. I think that his concerns meant clearly defining the elements so that there isn't uncertain or whimsical application. The necessity defense is a remarkable item in the law. It's that part of the law that says that there are more important things in this world than obeying the law; and it's probably the law's first line of defense against the charge of being called an ass.

Although the elements have to be carefully defined and clearly defined, the necessity defense can't be so narrowly defined as to lose its applicability to many different types of situations. We think that the Defendants can make it with the jury under the defense as it's outlined, and as it's worded generally in the *Warshow* and *Shotton* opinions; but the terms ought to be, I think, carefully elaborated by the Court in light of the particular claim of necessity that's being made here. So, we're asking in our request to charge that imminence be defined in accordance with the evidence here to stop an ongoing state of affairs. I think that's well within the intention of the defense.

We have had testimony here that thirty bodies turn up every day in the streets of El Salvador, and that may have been happening for years and it may go on for years; and yet an act of sincere conscious protesting, and trying to protect the next thirty, certainly ought to be within the jury's province to find justified by necessity.

THE COURT: Well, of course if the courts apply it appropriately and not inappropriately, there is the protection. I think the precedence is very instructive that way.

What about the comment of Chief Justice Barney as well, with regard to the fact that in *Warshow* the allegedly threatened harm was an ongoing, long-term problem. The development of nuclear power in that particular case, it wasn't a single threatening, imminent emergency because it was ongoing. Certainly your evidence indicates that the problems in Nicaragua and El Salvador are an historical parallel in terms of time. Why doesn't the same application that Chief Justice Barney made to nuclear power problems in

Warshow apply here as well?

MR. NELSON: I think that there is an instructive comparison to be made. The issue in *Warshow* was the effect of low-level radiation. It was alleged to be accumulatively lethal perhaps, and yet there was no evidence. And I don't think there could have been any offer of evidence that the next day's dosage, or the next minute's dosage presented a risk of the sort of harm which the necessity defense allows people to protect other people against.

I think that the case would have been quite different if there had been a supported offer of proof that the radiation being emitted from that plant was killing people every day.

THE COURT: Was it decided before or after Three Mile Island, by the way?

MR. NELSON: Before it.

THE COURT: Yes; I think that's significant, too.

MR. NELSON: Yes, it is, but I would offer this hypothetical proposal which isn't all that far-fetched, in light of the evidence we heard.

Let's suppose that we have a murderer shooting a line of people, one after the other. It's a long line; it's been going on for years, and it stretches ahead for years. If somebody in an act of conscience breaks the law to try to stop the execution of those uncounted people, he or she ought to be able to justify any transgression of law on the basis of the necessity defense. We think that that's our case.

THE COURT: Very well. Also, I have another concern. I have referred a couple of times to former Chief Justice Barney's opinion in *Warshow*; the query is: is *Warshow* still law in Vermont, in view of the *Shotton* opinion. I note that Mr. Justice Peck, in the subsequent opinion in *Shotton*, cites favorably Chief Justice Billings' dissent in *Warshow*. Is the dissent of former Justice Billings now the law in view of *Shotton* or is *Warshow* still the law?

MR. NELSON: I think actually that the dissent of Justice Billings was always the law, that there really wasn't substantial disagreement in the Court that proof of some evidence on each of the elements of the defense ought to require the Court to charge the defense to the jury. I think the real difference in *Warshow* was whether some evidence had been produced on all points. I think that the subsequent opinion in *Shotton* indicates that the Court takes a fairly generous view to offers of this sort, and feels in general that when people differ about the evidence as to the reasonable actions of the Defendants, it ought to be given to a jury.

THE COURT: What do you say about Justice Hill's concurring opinion in *Warshow* that there is an exception to the necessity defense whereby legislative determination of informational policy precludes submitting the balancing values question to the jury. Is that the law and does it apply here?

MR. NELSON: In response, I am answering no to both. It's certainly not the holding of the Court. It's a separate basis that Justice Hill has for joining the majority. The Court has never said that. So it's an opinion of one Justice. It's not the law of this State.

I argue secondly, that if this is a legal principle which you can rely on, it doesn't apply here. You've got evidence that the goings on in Central America are really not the product of a deliberate legislative decision or even of a proper executive decision. Testimony was received that the CIA is totally responsible for policy tactics in the region. And testimony from Professor Rosenberg, I remember, indicated also that it was low-level people, or at most, cabinet-rank people who were the major officials supporting the sort of atrocities that our clients have tried to prevent. And so this isn't actually a set and promulgated government policy. It's a policy of a faction of government.

The fact that these people hold office, even that they hold high office, certainly can't immunize them from actions which would be proper if directed against crimes committed by people of lowlier rank.

THE COURT: Well, thank you. Ms. Shingler, would you like to follow up any of those matters?

MS. SHINGLER: Yes, I would, Your Honor. I would urge the Court to adopt the interpretation of imminence in *Warshow*, although I do believe the *Shotton* Court does modify the necessity defense, turning it from an objective to a subjective standard. I do not see anything in *Shotton* that changes the definition or the explanation of imminence that appears in *Warshow*. I believe that that is —

THE COURT: Well, didn't Mrs. Shotton have what you and I might conceive of as reasonable alternatives available to her, too? She called an ambulance.

MS. SHINGLER: Apparently not. She was in the process of being assaulted by her husband and I don't think it would be reasonable to ask anybody who was in the middle of an assault within her home to stick around and make a phone call. My understanding of the facts in *Shotton* indicates that she was running to get help after a brawl between herself and her husband, and I think it would be truly unreasonable to ask her to stick around and wait for an ambulance to show up. It was indicated in the facts of the case that she felt that she had no reasonable alternative and I think that was very clear. The woman suffered severely in terms of her injuries.

THE COURT: She had a number of broken ribs, yes.

MS. SHINGLER: A number of broken ribs, that's correct. And I think it would be absolutely unreasonable to say that she did have an alternative of sticking around and waiting for an ambulance. By the time the ambulance got there, it may have been too late. She should maybe call the coroner. I don't think that that's —

THE COURT: Did she have a reasonable alternative instead of driving drunk all the way to the hospital, of driving drunk just to the nearest house where there were lights on and getting help?

MS. SHINGLER: I'm not sure if there were lights on in any of the neighboring houses. That factual situation is unclear in the appellant's opinion. Maybe those alternatives were not available to her. I'm not familiar with the neighborhood in which Mrs. Shotton lived, and it could have been a very rural neighborhood as many neighborhoods are in this State.

It's possible that she felt that she had to get further away from her home than simply the neighbors. This man apparently was out to kill her, and I think that given the seriousness of the assault that it was extremely reasonable for her to get in her car and get out of there as far and as fast as she could go.

THE COURT: Well, the *Shotton* case law indicates that we have to balance the value of the alleged action only in terms of combating a serious harm which was perceived by the Defendants against the seriousness of the offense, the technical offense which was committed. And in weighing those, isn't the conduct of Mrs. Shotton driving drunk far more threatening to public safety and public order than an unlawful trespass in a public office? She could have called somebody.

MS. SHINGLER: You certainly could speculate on that. I do not believe that we have, for example, her BAC level, or how intoxicated she was.

THE COURT: I believe the officer indicated that her driving was pretty erratic. That does appear in Justice Peck's opinion. I mean Mrs. Shotton could have killed somebody.

MS. SHINGLER: But she didn't. And she could have been killed herself, and that was far less speculative. It was an imminent, compelling emergency. She was going to get killed. She was nearly killed.

THE COURT: Right, but also her conduct was much more egregious, was it not?

MS. SHINGLER: I do not think so, Your Honor.

THE COURT: Driving drunk is less serious than —

MS. SHINGLER: Than being killed.

THE COURT: I'm comparing the harm of the offense here. Driving drunk is less serious than an unlawful trespass in the Senator's office?

MS. SHINGLER: It's our position that there is no real emergency here, whereas there was one in *Shotton*. I would like to explain. Throughout the testimony that we've heard, the Defendants over and over again have stated that they were not there to stop the killing in Central America on March 26th. They were there to educate the Senator. The State submits to the Court, Your Honor, that Senator Stafford's lack of education is not a compelling and imminent emergency.

THE COURT: What about the Camden 28 trial where the court there obviously submitted necessity to the jury and informs it in terms of the Vietnam War?

MS. SHINGLER: Yes. There appears to be no uniformity as to the necessity defense among jurisdiction even in the Atlantic seaboard states. We have seen that in New Hampshire and Vermont very significantly. We also see that within the last couple of years, Vermont itself has taken a different position. I don't think it's correct to use New Jersey law in Vermont District Court at this time when we have Vermont law to deal with.

THE COURT: Very well. Any other of the issues that Mr. Nelson and I discussed that you want to follow up on?

MR. BRADLEY: I would like to add one thing that I don't believe Mr. Nelson has addressed in his oral argument and that is the nexus argument. I think there has to be some reasonable expectation that what the Defendants chose to do has some possibility of averting the emergency, if it is deemed to be an emergency, and I believe that sitting in Senator Stafford's office is about as far away as you can get from stopping the killing in Central America. There simply is no logical reason, nexus between the emergency —

THE COURT: Wasn't that the thrust of Dr. Zinn's testimony this morning?

MR. BRADLEY: Well, I would submit to the Court that he said that that was one alternative. And that he posited several alternatives, including draft resistance; that's another alternative available today, now with the re-signing-up. He talked about gathering in the vets. He talked about a variety of alternatives, and I would submit to you that though he did say that sitting-in may at some point down the line have a logical nexus, it was my opinion of — my interpretation of Mr. Zinn's testimony, that he was talking about a package deal, all of which is under the title of civil disobedience.

THE COURT: In view of the one incident alone, however, as I understood the thrust of Dr. Zinn's testimony and Mr. Countryman's testimony, as well as the testimony of some of the Defendants over the past couple of days, this was part of a nationwide effort. Can we look at this incident out of the context of other efforts?

MR. BRADLEY: Well, I think it's a no-win situation for the Defendants, Your Honor, based on Dr. or Mr. Zinn's testimony, in that even if it was a broad picture, one part of a series, I think that that gives more credence to the State's argument that there were reasonable alternatives, that there were ten things that were going on: protesting, drives, letter drives, etc., etc., etc, one facet of that being unlawfully trespassing.

I have not heard any testimony that if they had chosen to omit the violation of the unlawful trespass statute, and continue in their zealous pursuit, those nine or eight other alternatives, that whatever they sought to achieve would be achieved in any lesser sense.

THE COURT: Would you have prosecuted the people who were responsible for the Boston Tea Party for unlawful trespass?

MR. BRADLEY: I don't really prosecute anybody. Well, it's not my decision.

THE COURT: You are the spokesman at the moment.

MR. BRADLEY: Yes. I believe that that is a hypothetical that I'm not willing to address at this time. However, I would like to point out to the Court that —

THE COURT: Well, it's very similar, isn't it?

MR. BRADLEY: No, I disagree, Your Honor. That was part of a revolution that was intending to overthrow the government.

THE COURT: It was prior to the revolution.

MR. BRADLEY: Well, my sense of American history perhaps is a little confused, but it was my understanding through Mr. Zinn's testimony that it was. He discussed the Boston Tea Party and certain other acts of disobedience of the colonists in the context of American Revolution. It is my understanding that the Defendants weren't trying to overthrow the American government. I have not heard anything indicating that they were out to overthrow the American government, and, therefore, I think it's clearly distinguishable from this case; and, therefore, I choose not to address that hypothetical.

THE COURT: Very well. Mr. Nelson?

MR. NELSON: I never heard, Your Honor, that the intention to overthrow the government was an element of necessity defense. If it is, we haven't met it.

People have been handing me notes on the major question which the State is addressing, that is, the existence of reasonable alternatives.

I'd like to point out that this case involves two of the crucial underpinnings of American democracy; on the one hand, the right to petition and to public debate with one's representatives, and the accountability of one's representatives. And on the other hand, the right to a jury trial.

I think that the Defendants have testified that there was no alternative to open debate in this case.

THE COURT: As they perceived it.

MR. NELSON: As they perceived it; as they reasonably perceived it. I think to take that question away from the jury, to say to the jury it's not for you to decide, is to deny democracy.

Another basis for our claim of no alternatives to what happened rests on the imminence of the crucial vote in the Senate. The timing of this demonstration wasn't random. It was part of a coordinated nationwide effort, and it was timed to coincide with crucial legislative developments.

THE COURT: Can I have a moment? Essentially what you're saying, Mr. Nelson, the Defendants testified that they did perceive that there was no alternative available to them; and that the question of their credibility and the question of the reasonableness of their perception, are classic jury questions.

MR. NELSON: That's exactly it. I don't think that I have anything more to argue on that point.

THE COURT: Ms. Shingler?

MS. SHINGLER: Yes, Your Honor. It's unfortunate that the jury may not get the instruction as to the necessity defense. Perhaps they would get confused as to why this testimony existed. However, the Court has to follow the state of the law as it is today, and *Shotton* clearly says that if there is not some evidence as to the four elements, it cannot go to the jury. I would implore the Court to follow *Shotton*'s decision in that respect.

THE COURT: I will do my best.

MS. SHINGLER: I'm sure you will. I just wanted to point out with respect to the Boston Tea Party hypothetical, it's my understanding they would have been found guilty of breaking the law if they were prosecuted. And I think that's a salient point to the hypothetical.

THE COURT: You would have prosecuted them and convicted them?

MS. SHINGLER: Hypothetically, Your Honor.

THE COURT: Very good. We do have direct testimony on the element you're challenging in the form of testimony of the Defendants. They testified that they perceived no alternative; and isn't the question of whether or not they're testifying truthfully and the question of whether or not that perception, if the jury choses to believe their testimony was or was not reasonable, isn't that up to the jury?

MR. BRADLEY: No, Your Honor, I would disagree. I would feel that throughout their testimony, even though there were indications that they perceived no other alternative, they in fact got up on the stand and told us and the jury the very reasonable alternatives that they had pursued: Witness for Peace, the letter campaign, the variety of political campaigns that they did with respect to Senator Stafford in particular, and across New England in general. I think Witness for Peace, which we heard about, was a clear and reasonable alternative that many of the Defendants apparently undertook.

I think it's a contradiction of their testimony to say that they perceived no other alternative after they have sat there for a half hour and told us about the many different, reasonable alternatives that they have undertaken in the past, and plan on undertaking in the future.

THE COURT: That's a clear credibility argument. Whether or not they are to be believed isn't for me to presume to decide; it's for a jury to decide.

MR. BRADLEY: I believe that the simple association by the Defendants in light of all the other contradictory evidence, is sufficient to satisfy the no reasonable alternative element of the necessity defense.

THE COURT: So I should find as a matter of law, that they're testifying falsely?

MR. BRADLEY: No, I do not think that satisfies the burden of some evidence. One statement out of some others that contradicts that one statement, does not satisfy the criteria of some evidence. I'm not suggesting the Defendants are lying. I'm not asking the Court to find that they are lying. I have never once suggested that. What I'm saying is that there is not adequate evidence to give to the jury.

THE COURT: If it were an objective test I think that might be clear, but it's a subjective test. I think you agree with that?

MR. BRADLEY: Reluctantly so, yes.

THE COURT: You have to follow *Shotton*, too.

MR. BRADLEY: I am aware of that.

THE COURT: Very well, anything further, Mr. Nelson, on that issue?

MR. NELSON: No, Your Honor.

Appendix

The Necessity Defense in Political Trials: An Appraisal

by Linda L. Vance, Esq.

I.

In 1908, the Vermont Supreme Court was presented with a novel issue: Could the owner of a boat, endangered by a sudden storm on Lake Champlain, be justified in trespassing on the lands of another to save his own life and those of his passengers? The Court responded affirmatively; faced with imminent danger, and having a choice between suffering it or breaking the law to avert it, a person has a legal right to choose the lesser harm (*Ploof v. Putnam* , 81 Vt. 471, 71 A. 188 (1908)).

In 1984, in the trial of the "Winooski 44," a Chittenden County jury faced a much different issue: Could individual citizens, believing that their government's actions in Central America endangered the lives of inhabitants of that region, be justified in trespassing in a U.S. Senator's office to persuade him to vote against increased military aid to the Nicaraguan contras? Again, the response was affirmative; the jury acquitted twenty-six people of the charges against them (*State v. Keller et al.*, Docket No. 1372-4-84 CnCr.; *Barre-Montpelier Times Argus*, November 17, 1984).

Despite the great gulf of time and context between the two decisions, they are united in law by virtue of both being applications of the so-called "necessity" or "choice of harms" defense. Known to the Common Law since the sixteenth century, the defense has been recognized in U.S. criminal actions since at least 1810, when a federal court held that a ship was entitled to seek refuge in a foreign port in violation of embargo laws to preserve the lives of its crew and passengers (*The William Gray*, 29 F. Cas. 1300 (C.C.D.N.Y. 1810)). It has been held to justify crimes as varied as possession of marijuana (*United States v. Randall*, 104 Daily Wash. L. Rep. 2249 (D.C. Super. Ct. 1976)), leaving the scene of an accident (*Woods v. State*, 135 Tex. Crim. 540, 121 S.W. 2d 604 (1938)), escaping from prison (*State v. Horn*, 58 Hawaii 452, 566 P.2d 1378 (1978)) and mutiny (*United States v. Borden*, 24 F. Cas. 1202 (D.C. Mass. 1857)), and while there are no reported instances, there is *dicta* to the effect that it could be raised against a charge of homicide (*United States v. Holmes*, 26 F. Cas. 366 (C.C.E.D.Pa. 1842)). In 1958, it was incorporated into the Model Penal Code, and has since been adopted in that form, or one closely resembling it, by a large number of states. The rest, including Vermont, have continued to rely on the Common Law characterization of the defense, while sometimes looking to Model Penal Code-based precedents for elaboration of specific elements.

There have been relatively few opportunities for the Vermont Supreme Court to rule on the necessity defense in a criminal law context. In a way, this is fortunate; the defense has suffered considerably from *ad hoc* interpretations in other jurisdictions, but due to its rarity has evolved uniformly in Vermont. In each of the three cases which presented a plea of necessity to the Supreme Court, the same formulation of its elements was adopted:

> (1) There must be a situation of emergency arising without fault on the part of the actor concerned;
>
> (2) this emergency must be so imminent and compelling as to raise a reasonable expectation of harm either directly to the actor or upon those he was protecting;
>
> (3) this emergency must present no reasonable opportunity to avoid the injury without doing the criminal act; and
>
> (4) the injury impending from the emergency must be of sufficient seriousness to outmeasure the criminal wrong.

(*State v. Warshow*, 138 Vt. 22, 24, 410 A.2d 1000, 1001-1002 (1980); *State v. Shotton*, 142 Vt. 558, 560-561, 458 A.2d at 1105 (1983); *State v. Dapo*, 143 Vt. 610, 614, 470 A.2d 1173, 1177 (1983). These same elements were charged to the jury, with only minor changes in wording, in the *Keller* case: see *State v. Keller, Portion of Jury Charge in Trial by Jury*, p. 6.)

In two of these cases — *Shotton* and *Dapo* — the Court agreed on the application of the defense as well as the interpretation. Both cases involved convictions for operating a motor vehicle while under the influence of intoxicating liquor (DUI), and in both cases defendant-appellants argued that the trial court had erred in failing to instruct the jury on the necessity defense. In *Shotton*, the defendant claimed that she had been driving to the hospital to seek medical care for injuries inflicted upon her in an assault by her husband; she testified at trial that she had no phone, that her husband had been drinking heavily, and that she had been unwilling to walk to the neighbors' homes for help in case no one was there — in short, that the only way for her to deal with the emergency was to commit the wrongful act. A unanimous court held that the defense should have gone to the jury.

Dapo presented a somewhat different fact pattern. Defendant, having been informed by his ex-wife that their son was missing, went to search for him in his car. He found the boy, dropped him at the mother's house, and was returning home when he was apprehended by police. Again the Court was unanimous, this time in agreeing that while a lost child might constitute an emergency within the definition of necessity, any such emergency had already ended by the time Dapo was arrested.

While the use of the necessity defense in DUI cases has been a matter of some dispute in other jurisdictions — many courts have held that self-induced intoxication constitutes "fault" within the meaning of the first element and therefore precludes the defense — it seems apparent that situations such as that in *Shotton* are paradigmatic "proper" uses. The same may be said of a number of other hypothetical examples often advanced to explain necessity; violating speed limits to drive an injured child to a doctor, for instance, or breaking into a burning building to rescue someone trapped inside. In all these cases, the technical violation of the law seems somewhat beside the point. It is the less clear-cut cases, and particularly those involving protests or acts of civil disobedience, which so many observers find disquieting, and which generate conflicting opinions.

The acquittal of the "Winooski 44" in *Keller* produced a flurry of letters, editorials and critical responses in the press, and provided a topic of debate for judges and academics. Some commentators offered dire predictions that the case would pave the way for any and all politically disaffected groups to "take the law into their own hands" (Editorial, *Burlington Free Press*, November 16, 1984); others assailed the defendants, attorneys and witnesses involved in the case for making "a mockery of our system" (Letter to the Editor, *Barre-Montpelier Times Argus*, November 30, 1984).

These reactions to *Keller* were not particularly novel, either in Vermont or elsewhere. *State v. Warshow*, a 1980 Vermont case arising from protests at the Vermont Yankee Nuclear Power Corp. plant, produced similar concerns, even though the defendants were ultimately unsuccessful in their attempts to justify their actions with a plea of necessity. In affirming their convictions, Justice Hill wrote:

> If we were to allow defendants to present the necessity defense . . . we would, in effect, be allowing a jury to redetermine questions of policy already decided by the legislative branches of the federal and state governments. This is not how our system of government was meant to operate. (*Warshow*, at 28.)

Echoing in his remarks are the doctrines of judicial restraint from the public law arena: political questions, standing, equitable discretion. All, in effect, proclaim policy disputes between citizens and government, between the legislature and the executive, to be inappropriate for judicial resolution. What becomes apparent in *Warshow*, and decisions like it, is that the judiciary's reluctance to challenge the apparently valid activities of other branches of government often leads judges to look beyond the facts of a given case and to speculate on the impact on society *as a whole* if the necessity defense were routinely admitted.

Justice Hill's *caveat* about the workings of our system of government is much more subdued than the ominous warnings of judges in other jurisdictions, who often express fears that the necessity defense, if accepted in political cases, will open a floodgate of disrespect for the law. For example, in *United States v. Moylan* (417 F.2d 1002 (1969), *cert. denied* 397 U.S. 910 (1970)), the Fourth Circuit Court of Appeals, affirming defendants' conviction for destroying Selective Service records, stated:

> No legal system could long survive if it gave every individual the option of disregarding with impunity any law which by his personal standard was judged morally untenable. Toleration of such conduct would be democratic . . . but inevitably anarchic. (At 1009.)

An even greater degree of distaste was expressed by the Seventh Circuit in *United States v. Cullen* (454 F.2d 386 (1971)), which dealt with similar facts. Rejecting defendant's necessity plea, the Court declared:

> [Anyone] who elects to serve mankind by taking the law into his own hands thereby demonstrates his conviction that his own ability to determine policy is superior to democratic decision making. [His] professed unselfish motivation, rather than a justification, actually identifies a form of arrogance which organized society cannot tolerate. (At 392.)

How valid are these concerns? Is there a real danger that judicial acceptance of the necessity defense in political cases would lead to generalized disrespect for the rule of law and a rash of law-breaking by individuals? The balance of this essay will show that quite the opposite is true; that the necessity defense, given the stringency of its elements, is available in only a narrow range of cases and in those furthers both the purposes of the criminal law and the basic principles of organized society.

II.

Critics fear that the necessity defense could be employed to justify any type of protest. If necessity can be used by anti-intervention protestors who occupy a senator's office, could it not also be used by anti-abortion groups which occupy or even bomb family planning clinics? If the defense can be raised by persons charged with blocking access to nuclear power plants or weapons factories, would it not also be available to those who attempt to damage or destroy such plants or their equipment? Would it work for creationists who disrupt classrooms where evolution is taught? Or for animal liberation adherents who remove or destroy leg-hold traps on another's land?

In fact, there are few recorded instances of the necessity defense succeeding in political cases. In part, of course, this is due to the nature of our case reporting system — acquittals at trial level rarely leave a published record — but more importantly it is because the defense's elements are so difficult to satisfy, even when liberally interpreted.

The first element — that there be a situation of emergency arising without fault on the part of the actor — is in general the easiest requirement to meet. Fault, problematic in many conventional cases, is rarely at issue in political ones, and the harms which defendants have typically attempted to forestall — nuclear war, murder of civilian populations, etc. — are easily categorized as "emergencies." Moreover, the emergency need not *in fact* exist; defendants must show only that they reasonably *believed* it to exist. Nonetheless, the requirement of reasonableness does preclude the use of the necessity defense by "crack-pots" whose beliefs have no basis in objective fact (*Comm. v. Capitolo*, 421 A.2d 462 (Pa. 1984)).

The second requirement — that the emergency be so imminent and compelling as to raise a reasonable expectation of harm — was the one the majority in *Warshow* found the defendants unable to satisfy. The defendants contended at trial that their attempt to block workers' access to the nuclear power plant (which had been shut down for refueling and repair) was motivated by a fear that a nuclear meltdown would occur upon start-up. However, a majority of the Supreme Court characterized their claim differently. Finding that defendants' offer of proof established only that they had wanted to call attention to the dangers of low-level nuclear radiation, nuclear waste and nuclear accident, it ruled that such long range hazards could not constitute "imminent" danger, but were instead "speculative and uncertain." (*Warshow* at 25.) While the emergency need not be geographically close, and may be ongoing, such as the Central American "emergency" was in *Keller*, it must be "near at hand" and threatening; in short, it must be such that time permits few options.

It is the third element of the necessity defense — that the emergency must present no reasonable opportunity to avoid it without doing the criminal act — which mitigates against the success in political cases. In the *Keller* case, the "Winooski 44" went to great pains to show that they had exhausted attempts to influence Senator Stafford through normal channels: letters, phone calls, requests for public meetings, etc. Moreover, reports of testimony offered during the trial indicate that they believed Senator Stafford's vote to be pivotal on a pending Senate proposal to resume aid to the contras, and further believed the occupation of this office to be the only alternative open to them (*Burlington Free Press*, November 17, 1984). Part of the "Winooski 44's" success was attributed to Judge Mahady's ruling that the burden of proof shifted to the prosecution once some evidence had been adduced on each element of the defense (*Barre-Montpelier Times Argus*, November 17, 1984), but it would seem that even when the burden shifts — which is rare — prosecutors can easily prove the existence of alternatives. In case after case, courts have held that other avenues were open for political protesters to challenge or "prevent" threatened harm:

> There are thousands of opportunities for the propagation of the defendants' message: in the nation's electoral process; by speech on public streets, in parks, in auditoriums, in churches and lecture halls; and by the release of information to the media, to name only a few. (*United States v. Quilty*, 741 F.2d 1031 at 1033 (7th Cir. 1984)).

In addition to showing an absence of alternatives, defendants are also often required to establish that the action they chose was reasonably calculated to avoid the harm. (*State v. Keller, Portion of a Jury Charge in Trial by Jury*, p. 8. Although Judge Mahady instructed this as a part of the fourth element, it more accurately speaks to the question of alternatives.) Given the often symbolic nature of political protest, this requirement is rarely satisfied, unless the harm to be avoided is narrowly construed by the defendants and the actions they take are pointed and appropriate. The Pennsylvania case of *Commonwealth v. Berrigan* (472 A.2d 1099 (Pa. Super. 1984)) and the *Keller* case offer rare examples of political defendants being able to overcome this "causality" hurdle. In *Berrigan*, the Superior Court of Pennsylvania considered whether beating on missile components with hammers could avert nuclear war. Noting that the defendants' expert testimony, excluded at trial, was designed to show that the damaged components were vital parts of nuclear weapons, the majority held that "the argument might reasonably be made that the destruction of these components could avert nuclear disaster to an appreciable degree." (At 1107.) In *Keller*, testimony offered by defendants indicated that they believed their occupation of

Senator Stafford's office would influence him to vote against aid to the contras, which would in turn alleviate suffering and destruction in Nicaragua (*Barre-Montpelier Times Argus*, November 17, 1984). Had they taken the same action when a vote was not imminent, or had they occupied a place not so intimately tied to law-making as a senator's office — say, for example, the post office — the causal link would have been more difficult to claim.

Certainly, it has been the inability to establish that link which has led to the failure of the necessity defense in most political cases. For example, in *United States v. Dorrell* (758 F.2d 427 (9th Cir. 1985)), the Court held that spray-painting government property could not reasonably be expected to lead to the abandonment of the MX missile program or the avoidance of nuclear catastrophe. Similarly, burning of Selective Service records was held to be an insufficient means of stopping the progress of the Vietnam War (*United States v. Simpson*, 450 F.2d 515, 518 (9th Cir. 1972)); strewing blood and ashes on the walls of the Pentagon lacked the capacity to effect a change in U.S. weapons policy (*United States v. Cassidy*, 616 F.2d 101, 102 (4th Cir. 1979)); and demonstrating at a plant manufacturing nuclear weapon components offered no real likelihood of preventing the use or threat of nuclear weapons (*United States v. Linnehan*, 454 So. 2d 625 (Fla. 1984)).

The fourth element of the defense — that the injury sought to be avoided outweighs the defendant's crime — does not at first blush hinder political defendants. Who would argue that trespass is a greater harm than a nuclear accident or the death and suffering attendant to war? This is especially true for defendants who can assert that the harm they were decrying was itself illegal. The "Winooski 44", for example, relied heavily on the argument that the government's actions in Central America were contrary to international law (*Barre-Montpelier Times Argus*, November 13, 1984). However, in many situations the use of the necessity defense will be altogether precluded by a "legislative value choice" which is itself valid, i.e. neither unconstitutional nor at odds with international law. This subcondition appears to originate in the Model Penal Code's definition of necessity, which includes as an element a requirement that "a legislative purpose to exclude the justification does not otherwise plainly appear." Common Law jurisdictions frequently incorporate the subcondition in their definitions as well, and in *Warshow*, both Justice Hill and Justice Billings referred to it as part of accepted law. For Justice Hill, the existence of numerous state and federal laws promoting the development and regulation of nuclear power implied "the policy choice that the benefits of nuclear energy outweigh the dangers." (*Warshow* at 28; see also *State v. Dorsey*, 118 N.H. 844, 846, 395 A.2d 855 (1978)).

Of course, the mere fact that a legislative scheme of regulation exists should not preclude the defense in all cases. Emergency situations can result from oversights in regulatory schemes or from non-compliance with rules (*Silkwood v. Kerr-McGee Corp.*, 104 S.Ct. 615, 625, 78 L.Ed.2d 443 (1984)). But generally speaking, the existence of clear-cut and legal governmental policy will prevent the plea's success, and the same would be true if the policy determination had been made by the courts through constitutional interpretation. Thus, in the case of anti-abortion demonstrators occupying a clinic, while protestors might be able to show a reasonable belief that they were using the only means possible to prevent "injury" to the fetuses being aborted, they would not be able to surmount the effect of *Roe v. Wade* (410 U.S. 113, 93 S.Ct. 705, 35 L.Ed.2d 147 (1973)) and *Planned Parenthood of Central Missouri v. Danforth* (428 U.S. 52, 96 S.Ct. 2831, 49 L.Ed.2d 788 (1976)). Rejecting the necessity defense in *People v. Stiso* (416 N.E.2d 1209 (Ill. 1981)), the Appellate Court of Illinois stated:

> [T]he alleged injury sought to be avoided, the abortions, was not a legally recognised injury . . . . [T]he United States Supreme Court has upheld the right of women to obtain first trimester abortions without interference from spouses or parents. (At 1211; citations omitted.)

Given the stringency of the elements of the necessity defense, it seems clear that even the liberal interpretations will prompt only a trickle, not a flood, of successes in political trials. The remaining question, then, is whether it should *ever* be allowed to justify acts of disobedience and dissent.

III.

The essence of the necessity defense is that individuals are sometimes justified in breaking the law. It is this essence, rather than the stringency of the defense's elements, which is communicated by acquittals in highly publicized trials. Therefore, one might argue, the impact of the necessity defense may be vastly disproportionate to the frequency of its success; even the occasional acquittal might contribute to lawlessness or undermine the authority of lawful institutions. Certainly, this is the position taken by a number of judges quoted earlier. But does this argument have any merit?

I would answer that it does not. The criminal justice system, with or without a necessity defense, is generically unsuited to interaction with political protest. Its normative functions simply do not apply when people are acting out of conscience. Unless the defense were so often successful as to guarantee virtual immunity to all types of protesters — which we have seen is not the case — its availability will not incite the kind of rampant lawbreaking its critics fear. People who engage in acts of protest and civil disobedience are a rare breed (as anyone who has tried to organize even a benignly legal protest knows), and will do so whether or not they face punishment. Their motivation is political, and the personal consequences of their actions are of little concern to them. Some, in fact, may prefer incurring punishment to avoiding it, believing that this will underscore the depth of their opposition to the policies they protest. The notions of general and specific deterrence — supposedly the cornerstones of the criminal law — have little impact on intentional disobedience.

The concern that acquittals based on necessity will undermine the authority of lawful institutions is similarly misplaced. Indeed, the occasional success of a necessity plea may even enhance respect for the system. All constitutional democracies are predicated on an assumption that to be just, a government must create institutions which will correct its own injustices: The majority can be wrong. Thus, when application of a law to a particular fact situation would bring about an unfair result, the existence of the necessity defense allows an exception to be made. In that way, the defense offers an "escape hatch," a mechanism which creates specific openings in the sometimes monolithic structure of law and in so doing illuminates the law's overall justice and validity.

Of course, one might argue that there are sufficient opportunities to avoid injustice even without the necessity defense. In some cases, police will decline to arrest persons whose actions, though technically illegal, were necessary under the circumstances or were motivated by sincere moral conviction. Similarly, state's attorneys may waive prosecution, and judges may impose light or suspended sentences. Moreover, proponents of this view argue, legal professionals are well-equipped to make objective decisions. They are, after all, somewhat hardened by experience; they are less likely than jurors to be swayed by emotional rhetoric.

The problem with this argument is that police, prosecutors and judges, while perhaps immune to the moral appeals of political dissenters, are subject to mainstream public pressures in a way jurors are not. It is true that public opinion will often be indifferent, or even supportive, of political dissent. But it is equally true that when protest is directed at governmental policies, police are often urged to "crack down" on demonstrators by arresting them. So too, prosecutors may be admonished to "get tough" with protesters by pressing charges, and judges may be expected to "make examples" of them by meting out severe punishment.

Jurors, on the other hand, are not expected to account to the community for their actions; they *are* the community. As such, they can confine their deliberations to the facts and arguments of a particular case; they need not look to hypothetical long-range consequences of their decisions. In the exercise of their judgment, jurors are wholly unfettered by the pressures which limit other actors in the system.

But what of the pressures *within* the case? It seems that legal professionals are subjected to one kind of pressure, jurors to another. The impassioned rhetoric and highly-charged atmosphere of political trials cannot help but implicate jurors' emotions to some degree. The law, we are often told, should be opaque to moral arguments. Never mind that a person means well, or is acting out of moral convictions when breaking the law. The law must remain constant, must not yield to good intentions. If it does, its certainty and predictability will be lost.

This line of reasoning, however, argues for, rather than against, the necessity defense. Critics of the defense often assume that were it made unavailable in political cases, defendants would be unable to exert moral pressure on juries. But this is not always true. Political defendants often argue eloquently in support of their actions, even in cases where the defense has been excluded, and juries respond to that eloquence. While the law might not recognize discretion in juries, jurors themselves frequently discover it. If conscience compels them to nullify the operation of the law and acquit, they will do so, with or without a necessity defense, as happened in the recent trial of the "White Train" protesters in Seattle. Jury nullification, it would seem, is a far greater threat to lawful authority than a defense which permits value judgments only within a specific and well-defined framework.

Finally, we must remember that the necessity defense is not at the root of political protest. Exclude the defense, and the protest will continue unaffected. Allow it, and protesters will occasionally be able to demonstrate to juries that particular governmental policies create such danger, such an affront to peace and order, that immediate opposition is critical. But if it should ever happen that those who protest governmental policy are acquitted with regularity, we would do best to look to those policies, and not the necessity defense, for the cause.

First Place Winner, Vermont Bar Association Essay Contest, 1986

Reprinted by permission of
The Vermont Bar Journal & Law Digest
Volume 12, No. 2, April, 1986

Appendix

Resources for Information on Central America

American Friends Service Committee (AFSC)
Latin America Desk
1501 Cherry St.
Philadelphia, PA 19102
(215) 241-7000

Americas Watch Committee
36 West 44th St.
New York, NY 10036
(212) 840-9460

Center for Constitutional Rights
853 Broadway
New York, NY 10003
(212) 614-6464

Central America Education Fund
1151 Massachusetts Ave.
Cambridge, MA 02138
(617) 492-8699

Chicago Religious Task Force on Central America
407 S. Dearborn #370
Chicago, IL 60605
(312) 663-4398

Committee in Solidarity with the People of El Salvador (CISPES)
P.O. Box 50139
Washington, DC 20004
(202) 393-3370

Inter-Religious Task Force on Central America
475 Riverside Dr., Room 563
New York, NY 10115
(212) 870-3383

MADRE
5825 Telegraph Ave., Suite 55
Oakland, CA 94609
(212) 777-6470

Medical Aid to El Salvador
6030 Wilshire Blvd., #200
Los Angeles, CA 90036
(213) 937-3596

National Sanctuary Defense Fund
c/o Franciscan Friars of California
1610 Bush St.
San Francisco, CA 94109
(415) 474-5122

Network in Solidarity with the People of Guatemala (NISGUA)
930 F St. NW, Suite 720
Washington, DC 20004
(202) 737-6912

New El Salvador Today (NEST)
P.O. Box 4762
Berkeley, CA 94704
(415) 549-2114

Nicaragua Network
2025 I St. NW, Suite 1117
Washington, DC 20006
(202) 223-2328

North American Congress on Latin America (NACLA)
151 West 19th St., 9th Floor
New York, NY 10011
(212) 989-8890

Pledge of Resistance for Vermont/New Hampshire
Fran Nye
P.O. Box 260
Norwich, VT 05055
(802) 649-1687

Pledge of Resistance Hotline
Washington, DC
(202) 328-4042

Quest for Peace
Quixote Center
P.O. Box 5206
Hyattsville, MD 20782
(301) 699-0042

Witness for Peace
515 Broadway
Santa Cruz, CA 95060
(408) 425-3733

Witness for Peace New England Office
Fran Truitt
RD 2 Box 422A
Ellsworth, ME 04605
(207) 422-9007